THE CODE OF THE HEROIC SELF

(Note: This book will stare at you until you read it)

The Path

To Get

Everything You Want

Lives

Inside

THE CODE OF THE HEROIC SELF

SEVEN UNCONVENTIONAL TRUTHS TO TURN YOUR LIFE INTO YOUR BUSINESS & GET PAID TO BECOME YOUR BEST SELF

RYAN FLETCHER
FOUNDER OF STORYATHLETE

THE CODE OF THE HEROIC SELF
Seven Unconventional Truths To Turn Your Life Into Your Business & Get Paid To Become Your Best Self

© 2021 Ryan Fletcher.

All rights reserved. No portion of this book may be reproduced, stored in a retrieval system, or transmitted in any form or by any means—electronic, mechanical, photocopy, recording, scanning, or other—except for brief quotations in critical reviews or articles, without prior written permission of the author or publisher.

Published by IC® Publishing
Visit us online at StoryAthlete.com

Limit of liability / Disclaimer of Warranty: While the publisher and author have used their best efforts in preparing this book, they make no representations or warranties regarding the accuracy or completeness of the contents of this book. The publisher and author specifically disclaim any implied warranties or merchantability of fitness for a particular purpose and make no guarantees whatsoever that you will achieve any particular result. Any case studies that are presented herein do not necessarily represent what you should expect to achieve, since business success depends on a variety of factors. We believe all case studies and results presented herein are true and accurate, but we have not audited the results. The advice and strategies contained in this book may not even be suitable for your situation, and you should consult your own advisors as appropriate. The publisher and author shall not be held liable for any loss of profit or any other commercial damages, including but not limited to special, incidental, consequential, or other damages. The fact that an organization or website is referred to in this work as a citation and/or potential source of information does not mean that the publisher or author endorses the information the organization or website may provide or the recommendations it may make. It is sold with the understanding that the publisher is not engaged in rendering legal, accounting, or other professional services. If legal advice or other expert assistance is required, the services of a competent professional should be sought.

To my family, Melanie, Jackson and Zoey
I journey each day to become hard(er) to kill; mentally, physically and financially,
so that I can best serve you. I love you. You are the most important
piece of my life.

To my parents, Mom and Dad
For allowing me to fail, and not coddling me. And when I failed,
for always being there to support me.

To our StoryAthletes, the true guinea pigs;
Thank you for believing in me enough to test my concepts in your life,
across mind, body, business, relationships,
to discover what works and for sharing your breakthroughs
with every member of StoryAthlete.

CONTENTS

Before You Begin: Know This Is Not Your Typical Book - Page 9

Introduction: The 5-Part Crisis - Page 13

The Invisible Code: How Do We Change It? - Page 19

Our Greatest Achievement: Becoming A True Partner - Page 21

TRUTH #1: Inspiring Others Is A Real Profession (Transformation Drives Demand)
Where we learn how to create demand for our traveled path; people asking us "What's your secret?"

TRUTH #2: Leverage Partners (Business vs. Income)
Where we learn how to get paid to become our best self; delivering 3 types of value

TRUTH #3: Proven Frameworks (Combat Failure & Disease)
Where we learn how to combat FODQ, the main driver of failure, and the 3 negative cycles that feed it

TRUTH #4: Sacrifice Is Required (CRISPR: To Replace Defective Gene Sequences)
Where we learn how to "genetically engineer" our own genes; to destroy the Lesser Self

TRUTH #5: Harness Compounding (The Path To 37X Annual Growth)
Where we learn how to guarantee exponential growth through the aggregation of marginal gains; making failure impossible

TRUTH #6: Embedding In An Open Source (To Access Shared Breakthroughs)
Where we learn how to disrupt our own growth projections; innovating and achieving faster than we ever thought possible

TRUTH #7: It's Called The Hero's Journey (For Good Reason)
Where we learn how to connect "all the dots" to turn our Life into our business & Get Paid to become our best self

Don't Refuse The Call - Page 149

Heroic Self: StoryAthlete Partner? - Page 151

Resources: Stay Connected - Page 153

Note: This book should be read in the order the content is presented. If you read this book out of order, you will struggle to understand how to execute *the* Seven Truths.

Before You Begin: <u>Know</u> This Is Not Your Typical Book

In fact, I would be hesitant to call this a book at all. Most books purchased become little more than paperweights. Somebody felt ambitious in the moment. Got a recommendation from a friend, jumped on Amazon. Ordered. The book arrives. They're so excited it arrived; they quickly flip through it. From there, it sits on their counter or bedside, with the good intention of getting read, but it never does.

Which means, the world doesn't need another book. Another paperweight made out of paper. Ironic, right?

Books are full of information, but we already have too much information. Too much information is the source of our confusion. The source of our frustration. We are drowning in it. From being inundated on social media, to hundreds of 24-hour news networks. I would argue more information is the root cause of failure, and unhappiness, resulting in underachievement and depression. Information has become the cause of our overwhelm.

Overwhelm is what paralyzes us.

So I designed, then wrote this book to be something different. I provide very little information in this book. Information is about education. Traveling a path, on the other hand, is about movement. Momentum. Action. To change our life, we must change our actions. To change our actions, we must change our behaviors. To change our behaviors, we must change our beliefs. And to change our beliefs, we must change our stories. Easier said than done. If it were that easy, there would be no need for innovation or discovery or the search for a better way.

In this book, I present a challenging but tactical path. One, that if you follow, you will turn your Life into your business & get paid to become your best self. Work-life balance is a failed model. Entrepreneurs have tried to make it work for years. And failed for years. Work-life integration, for people like us, the 5% most ambitious, is the only path forward to achieve true happiness.

In addition to the tactical path presented in this book, where each *Truth* builds on the previous, let me explain some of the other abnormal facts and unique features:

ODD FORMATING:

We live in a world of chaos. The job of the human mind is to organize that chaos. It sifts and sorts through millions of data points, from incoming information, to make sense of the world. It organizes ideas into categories, then into subcategories. Then within those subcategories, it creates more subcategories. The brain, in doing this, is attempting to create a hierarchy of importance. What needs to be understood first, and then second, and then third. Likewise, the brain reads from left to right (and top to bottom) because we've trained it to read that way. And it uses a standard layout of indentation to know which subcategories belong to each category.

Indentation, in sense, is like a Russian Doll set.

The least indented section *is* the main category, then, each further indent going forward, in a cascading layout, is the subcategory that dives deeper into the presented idea. Normal books are about presenting information.

This book is about understanding and execution. The odd formatting is a way to help the brain to quickly organize the presented concepts, from big picture to small picture. This is a massive innovation in comprehension. By looking at any page, you can see the flow of importance.

DATA AND RESEARCH:

In my personal library, I have thousands of books on the topics of business, marketing, psychology, political science, written by radicals from both parties. And books on a dozen other topics.

Those books, different than this book, are loaded with academic research and citations. They present 50-pages of information to make a point that could be made in three sentences. I don't know about you, but I like the straight-shooter, no bullshit, insight gathered from real world experience, 3-sentence version that makes the point. Not the 50-page per point dissertation. Great insight isn't about length or format. Great insight is about belief, faith, and clarity.

As you read this book, you'll better understand the unique value of those three words: belief, faith, and clarity.

The best books I have read, enjoyed most, and have gotten the most out of, are those that document a first-hand account of the person's struggle. It could be the struggle of the author. Or the struggle of the person he observes. But in hearing the Journey of Struggle, I'm able to see, and experience, and learn, what it feels like (to be in the struggle) and what it takes (to escape the struggle.)

This book is the story of discoveries that I made while traveling the struggle. It is not a research paper. It is a field manual. And I am not an author in this book, I am a traveler on this journey with you.

COLLABORATION:

Like you, I'm an entrepreneur. Not an academic. Every day, I ask my kids a set of questions. Yes, I ask these questions to program their mind. But these questions go beyond that. It gets to a Code. A way of life.

The first question I ask: How do we get power? They answer, "By using our words." This continues. How do we become great? "By practicing." Do winners ever quit? "No." Do quitters ever win? "No." And, who makes money in this world? "Problem-solvers." Yes, problem-solvers. This is what entrepreneurship is about. We aren't innovators. We aren't visionaries. We aren't disruptors.

First, and foremost, we are problem solvers.

Solving a problem is the foundation to each of those previous titles. No disruptor became a disruptor by not solving a problem. No visionary became a visionary by not solving a problem. No innovator became an innovator by not solving a problem. Which brings into question, what problem needs to be solved to help people achieve their highest potential in life? To experience true happiness. And health. And financial security. Through executing their purpose, to become their best self…

Thankfully, I had access to hundreds of test subjects, inside of StoryAthlete, as my collaborators, to test and prove the *path* you'll read about in this book.

WRITING STYLE:

From start to finish, this is a first-hand account of my journey with everything I have learned, through the pain of my own struggle, and the struggle of our collaborators. At times, I swear and cuss. I don't use proper grammar or punctation. My writing style has been called strange, odd, even weird.

My focus is to convey the intent of the message, not on literary correctness.

My Mom is my editor. Is she a professional editor?

No.

I'm sure there are mistakes and errors. Misspelled words and wrong tenses. *Oh, well.* For me, writing is about the story and the connection to it. A shared journey. The act of discovering a new set of principles or beliefs.

If, at the end of this book, you feel, or say to yourself, "I like the way this guy thinks." Or you conclude, "This guy is on to something." Then I have succeeded. I won't win any Pulitzers in my lifetime.

But I may inspire millions to become *Harder(er) to kill; mentally, physically financially*, to best serve *those* they most love.

THE ONLINE EXPERIENCE:

This book comes with its own additional training, specific videos and tutorials to better demonstrate certain concepts presented within the book.

Access it from. www.StoryAthlete.com/heroic-book

CONNECT WITH ME:

I love being in touch with my fellow travelers. The struggle that we experience is what unites us all:

    Facebook.com/ryanfletcherhq
    Instagram.com/storyathletefletcher

MY WEB SITES:

To learn more about me and my work:

    StoryAthlete.com
    ImpactClub.com

OUR PODCAST:

Different than this book, the StoryAthlete Podcast is an ever growing and evolving version of the concepts presented here within. Join us. Tune-in. You will either love it or hate it. ;-)

    StoryAthletePodcast.com

Introduction: The 5-Part Crisis

> Many men die a good many years before the undertaker carts them away. A man begins to die when he ceases to grow.
>
> — W. E. Barton

The reason I wrote this book is because of the alarming number of people, and its increasing every day, that are depressed, frustrated, and unhappy with their current lot in life. Life isn't supposed to be this way. *What* went wrong? What am I *doing* wrong? What is *wrong* with me?

Many times, I have asked these questions. And wondered all these same thoughts. Our brain has this magical ability to create nightmares that terrify us, and fantasies that we can never live up to or achieve. And the worst part of this? Are the extremes that get built into these vivid imaginations. All or nothing. This creates the painful dystopia where, despite living in the most amazing time of our species' evolution, more people than ever are struggling to find their path and purpose in life.

Happiness, I would argue, is all that matters in our life. But happiness can't be achieved if we don't address this 5-part crisis.

THE FEAR-OF-FAILURE CRISIS:

A critical component of happiness is sustained growth and progress. As humans, we have this innate urge to continually grow. To achieve. To build bigger empires. To reach more people. To make a greater impact internally on the people we love, and externally, on our community. Legacy, living a *life* that matters, is a function of our ability to sustain progress. Continued growth.

The problem is. People's fear-of-failure is paralyzing. Start a new business. Launch a new marketing campaign. Start investing in real estate. *What if…, what if…, what if…,* the brain goes into hyperdrive imagining the worst possible outcome. Building a nightmare that terrifies us. This future reality, entirely *of our imagination,* convinces us that now is not the right time. I need to plan more. I need to prepare more. The risk is too great. The stakes are too high. Procrastination sets in.

Hesitation. Delay.

Two years pass, two decades pass, and people are *still* paralyzed. This creates a life of stagnation. A life of possibility becomes a life of mediocrity. No real progress. Stunted growth. And we're unhappy because inside we know we're capable of so much more. Our fear, though, perpetually defeats us. Fear-of-failure is a crisis of epic proportion. This *feeds* the underachieving crisis…

THE UNDERACHIEVING CRISIS:

Every human on earth, at some point, asks the question, "What is my purpose? Why am I here?" For many of us, as a parent and spouse, our greatest purpose is to serve our families. Financially. Emotionally. Spiritually. And to do so at the highest level, we realize we must be *superiorly* successful, financially, in mind and body, and in spirit. This is what gives us the mental focus and physical energy, the emotional capacity, financial resources, and finally, the time-availability to be "the rock" to *those* we love most. Mind. Body. Business. Relationships.

Alternatively, underachieving comes in many forms. You can have a 7-figure business but no time to be present in the moment with your kids. Or you can have six-pack abs but no financial resources to live beyond paycheck to paycheck.

Human beings are complex creatures.

Success and happiness in one-dimension (mind, or body, or business, or relationships) doesn't make up for underachieving in the other three. This creates a life of imbalance and unrest. To compensate, we put pressure on ourselves to achieve more. To achieve faster. *Faster, faster, faster!* This becomes the mantra.

Lose weight faster. Get stronger faster. Grow the business, faster. Which typically has the opposite effect. With greater pressure comes added stress and frustration. A stressed mind isn't an optimal mind. A stressed mind is a distracted and unfocused mind. And an unfocused mind is an unproductive mind. So, instead of achieving more. We achieve less. This *feeds* the unhappiness crisis…

THE UNHAPPINESS CRISIS:

Happiness is complex. It is a ghost. It can't be seen. It can only be felt and experienced. Further, it is the summation (happy vs. unhappy) of the complex matrix of everything happening in our lives. Too much salt, you ruin the cookies. Too much flour, the cookies aren't even cookies, they're bread. Happiness is the most complex recipe on earth. Mind. Body. Business. Relationships.

As such, tens of millions of people struggle to get it right. And, from the outside, even when the all the necessary ingredients look to be in place, the blueberry that may look blue on the outside, has been rotting from the inside. For the 5% most ambitious, this internal rotting happens to millions of us. We struggle to be content with any achievement we achieve. We should *be* happy. Most of the ingredients are in place. Maybe we have a great family. A great spouse. Amazing kids. We make a decent income. We have a nice house. Our loved ones are healthy. Check, check, check, and check. But yet, still, something festers inside. A gnawing dissatisfaction.

People tell us to be grateful. "You should be happy. Enjoy it. Celebrate your success." The problem is, they don't understand us. They don't get us. They don't know what drives us. We are outcasts to them. We feel like aliens. Why am I so different? We begin to question our purpose. We question our path. We question our identity. We question our abilities. It begins to feel like Us *vs*. The World. This unhappiness makes us desperate for change, but FUCK - we don't know *what* to change.

Out of time. Out of energy. Out of ideas.

At this point, we're just going through the motions of life. We aren't actually living. We certainly aren't thriving. And our loved ones, can see it. They can feel it. They try to help us. They want to help us. But their attempts to help us, because *they* don't understand us, because *we* don't even understand us, just annoys us. So, we begin to distance ourselves. We begin to hide. Both mentally and emotionally, we stop communicating. This *feeds* the depression crisis…

THE DEPRESSION CRISIS:

We find ourselves in this Dark place. Alone, annoyed, dissatisfaction still gnawing. The feeling of having no support and nobody to turn to for answers. Feeling lost is a painful reality. Who can help us? We've tried everything we know.

How do I *numb* the pain? A glass of wine, another beer. Two glasses of wine. 6 beers. How do I escape? How, for even a second, do I make the pain go away? More alcohol. Anti-depressants. Anti-anxiety medications. We medicate to sleep. We're stressed. We turn to food. Porn. We throw ourselves into our work, to isolate, to not deal with the relationships in our life. We're toxic.

Our attempts to communicate turn into fights. Turn into resentment. We say things we don't mean. In this toxic state, our attempts to make things better make things worse. So, we continue to turn inward. Further isolation. Less communication. Less motivation. Less drive. A scorched earth attitude develops.

"Fuck it. I don't care."

We further shutdown. We stop trying. We don't even attempt to care any longer. We feel foolish. We're embarrassed by our helplessness. We feel alone. Like that blueberry, we have rotted from the inside.

Externally, we still may appear to be that successful entrepreneur. But inside, and behind closed doors? We are painfully experiencing the collapse of our life. A shocking one in every six Americans is prescribed to some kind of anti-depressant. The depression *crisis* in our society is a tragedy of epic proportion.

What do we do about it? *What* is the root cause? *What* is the immediate and long-term answer?

THE LESSER SELF CRISIS:

This is the real crisis we must address.
This is the root cause.
The culprit.

Inside of all of us, there are two distinct beings. The Lesser Self vs. the Heroic Self. Each identity tells us what to do. Each has their own belief system. Like the devil and the angel, they sit on opposite shoulders as they whisper in our ears.

Do this. No, do that.

In a cascading effect, their voices dictate our results. Their differing stories create our beliefs. Those beliefs decide our behaviors. Our behaviors determine our actions. And our actions dictate our results.

These two voices, Lesser Self vs. Heroic Self, aren't just a battle of strength vs. weakness. Their stories dictate the outcome of our life. Which gets to society's greatest problem. The vast majority of people are Lesser Self-*dominated*. Meaning, in the tug-o-war battle of daily decisions, the easiest path is most often chosen. They place blame. They make excuses. They rationalize their shortcomings and weaknesses. They justify their failures. They hold high standards for others, but not themselves. They give up. They quit when shit gets hard.

They lack the commitment to stay the course. They start, they stop. They never continue. They start. Stop. Then delay.

They fear (and allow their fear) to paralyze their forward progress. They build no momentum. They sustain no progress. They lack confidence and self-esteem. They lack love for themselves. Their insecurities control their decisions. They project their insecurities onto others. Their self-worth plummets daily.

The *Lesser Self* is the worst Partner. The worst spouse. The worst parent. The worst friend. The worst child. The worst sibling. The worst boss. The worst employee. Of course, they don't see this negative side of themselves. Because the Lesser Self is a masterful negotiator. He creates the reality, in our head, he wants us to see. He can rationalize and justify even the weakest of traits. "Why do I need to change?! It's not my fault." Until the *Lesser Self* dies, nothing can stop the cascading *crisis* above...

SOLVING THIS 5-PART CRISIS:

By defeating the lead domino, in the *Lesser Self*, the root causes of fear, underachieving, unhappiness and depression, are defeated, too. When you finally become aware of the Lesser Self, and begin to see just how much his voice through the stories he tells, influences you.

You will come to *hate* that motherfucker.

You will want him dead, in the same way I wanted "Fat Ryan" and "All-Busines Fletcher," my Lesser Self, dead too.

For years, my Lesser Self destroyed my life. His weakness robbed me of progress. Robbed me of happiness. And destroyed my relationships.

He convinced me to believe in his stories. He didn't have my best interest at heart. He didn't care about me. Like a virus, and a host, as my *Lesser Self* grew inside and strengthened, my true self, my Heroic Self, slowly began to die.

I gained over 40-pounds.

I felt disconnected from my wife and kids. I threw myself into the business. I self-destructed. And I know, I'm not alone.

My struggle is the struggle of millions. Sadly, most people don't go in search of answers until they reach rock bottom. Hopefully, this book will reach them before they fall into that *darkest* pit.

This book is a *Light* to navigate out of, and away from, that Darkness. When we lose hope and our will to fight, the enemy is strengthened. If you give the Lesser Self an inch. He will take 9,000 miles.

```
Note: For many that are reading this. The concepts outlined
in this book will be the difference between life and death.
More than a dozen people have sent me letters and video
messages, telling me how StoryAthlete saved their life.
Suicide and depression, spurred on by fear,
underachievement and unhappiness, have become terrifying
epidemics.

    This is not just a book for you. This is a book for
    your family. Your friends. Your spouse. Your kids. And
    everyone who loves you. And that you love back. Only
    by defeating the Lesser Self, can we become a Light to
    others in the Dark. Our greatest gift; to others, and
    to our self, is the path of transformation that we
    create.

Buckle up.
```

The Invisible Code: <u>How</u> Do We Change It?

> Our beliefs are like unquestioned commands, telling us how things are, what's possible and impossible and what we can and cannot do. They shape every action, every thought, and every feeling that we experience. As a result, changing our belief systems is central to making any real and lasting change in our lives.
>
> — **Tony Robbins**

Did you read that Tony Robbins quote? Either way, read it again. Then I want you to read it once more. Now, read it again, except this time, read each sentence individually. Stopping and pausing after each part of the quote, to think about and dissect the actual meaning of each phrase.

What is *really* being said? "Our beliefs" "Unquestioned demands" "Telling us how things are" "What's possible and impossible" "What we can and cannot do" "They shape our every action..."

Now, put this in the context of the *Lesser Self*. "Our beliefs. Unquestioned demands. Telling us how things are. What's possible and impossible and what we can and cannot do. They shape our every action." And see, it's the last sentence of Robbin's quote that I want you to focus on. "As a result, changing our belief systems is central to making any real and lasting change in our lives." No shit, right? Everybody talks about the critical nature of mindset, and the importance of changing beliefs, but how can one change their beliefs if their beliefs are unquestioned commands? Do you really think the *Lesser Self* will allow you to change your beliefs? Willingly? Easily? Without a fight? You are asking the cancer that dominates your perspective, worldview, and decision-making, to please stop infecting you. Sorry, but cancer doesn't work that way. The *Lesser Self* is a fucking dictator, no different than Saddam Hussein. Stalin. Mussolini. Or Adolf Hitler. They made unquestioned commands, too. Those who questioned, were put to death. The *Lesser Self* doesn't care about you as a person, any more than the monsters I named cared about the human-life of their people, or the people they deemed their enemies and destroyed.

To remove a dictator from power, they must die or be killed. No dictator willingly gives up power. They wage war. And it isn't until someone rises up against them of greater strength, do they fall.

Your true self, your Heroic Self, I know would love to be the Commanding General responsible for toppling the empire of your *Lesser Self*. But your Heroic Self is a nice guy. And nice guys tend to finish last. That is, until nice guys grow a set of balls and stop fuckin' around.

In the pages of this book, you will find a blueprint to *defeat* the Lesser Self. It won't be easy. You can't just *think* happy thoughts. Or change your belief system by reading another self-help book.

I'm guessing you probably tried that already. How did it work?

I'm guessing it didn't.

You, no doubt, had good intentions. And you probably started off really strong. But within days, weeks, the *Lesser Self* was wiping the floor with your sorry ass. You started. You stopped. You quit. You started again. Then when Monday came around, and, for 58th week in a row, you said, "I'll start on Monday." "I'll do that tomorrow."

Well, guess what? That is your *Lesser Self* imposing his fucking will on you. You are his little bitch and he knows it.

What are you *prepared* to do about it?

Perhaps, just maybe, your Heroic Self has grown that set of balls and is done fucking around. If so, I know this position well. I was there. Fed up. My breaking point had been reached.

My *Lesser Self* had to die.

```
Note: To hear the full details of how this breaking point
was reached, listen to episode 1 of the StoryAthlete
Podcast.

     Listen at: StoryAthletePodcast.com
```

This will be fun.

This book is about winning *this* War.

Our Greatest Achievement: <u>Becoming</u> A True Partner

> StoryAthlete® is not just a company, podcast, or brand of T-shirt. It's a movement of changing the story we tell ourselves. Success is based on our beliefs. Our beliefs are based on the stories we tell ourselves. If we tell ourselves stories of self-defeat, as our Lesser Self, we destroy ourselves from within. Wherein destroying ourselves, we hurt and torture those closest to us.
>
> — **Ryan Fletcher**

When you live the *traits* that make you a great *Partner*, everyone wants to partner with you. As a spouse, you are a Partner. As a friend, you are a Partner. As a business owner and entrepreneur, you are a Partner. As a parent, you are a Partner. As a boss or employee, you are a Partner.

Great partnerships are built on the foundation of Character.

For this reason, the Lesser Self is the worst *Partner* in every respect. They will fail you. They won't do what they're supposed to do. Or what they agreed to do. They will quickly stab you in the back.

They will blame you.

They will claim to be one person in public but behave as another in private. They can't be trusted. They talk from both sides of their mouth. And when you need them most, they won't be there.

Further, as a *Partner*, your Lesser Self won't be *there* for you. When you need courage, he will give you cowardness. When you need strength, he will provide weakness. When you need discipline, he will provide excuses. When you need truth, he will provide justifications. When you need patience, he will demand instant gratification. And when you need to fight, he will quit.

The worst *Partner* you have in life is your Lesser Self. The worst part? He lives inside of you as a ruthless dictator.

The best *Partner* you can be to yourself, and to others, is your Heroic Self.

That's what this book is about.

StoryAthlete, not just this book, but this Community, is the path to guarantee that transformation.

    Note: We begin.

ESCAPE:
The Ordinary World

From Ryan Fletcher

StoryAthlete **PARTNER:**
The Chance to Rewrite the DNA of Your Life

CRISPR: If you want to change your world. You have to change how you see it. From this point forward, we shall see your *Life* as a string of DNA. To improve your DNA, we must knock out defective genes. And knock-in new superior genes. (Keep reading, there are 7 "gene sequences" that cause people to never live up to their potential in life. Should we replace these "gene sequences," with new superior "gene sequences", our potential gets achieved.)

Dear Friend,

Inside this book, I promise to show you how to turn your *LIFE* into your business. To get *PAID* to become your best self. StoryAthlete will even Partner with you. But neither Sloper, nor I, have any patience for the 95% who refuse to do what it takes to become great. *Greatness* is hard. *Greatness* is earned. *Greatness* requires sacrifice. This is what separates the 5% most ambitious.

Everybody wants to get rich by investing in real estate. They want to have endless deal flow. They want unlimited funding. They want to have superior relationships with other investors to partner with.

Everybody wants to enjoy the security of an *ultra*-profitable online business. They want to have mailbox money. They want to have automated marketing in place that makes sales while they vacation. They want to have recurring revenue. They want to be able to sleep at night, knowing they have financial security. (Financial stress, trust me I know, is a monster that rips apart and can destroy even the strongest person, marriage, or business. It's a stress that invades every aspect of our life. Hard to sleep. Hard to focus. Hard to concentrate. Hard to ever be present in the moment.)

Everybody wants to build a legacy for their kids, and spouse, and impact their community. They want to build a life they are proud of, where their spouse and kids are proud of them for building it. They want to be a superior financial provider. A superior role-model. They want to be able to deliver on their promises. (I can't even begin to enunciate how many fathers I know, that are ashamed and embarrassed by the fact they are mediocre providers. For so long, they have promised to their spouse, that things will "soon be different," and yet, year after year, investment after investment; in their business, in themselves, in another seminar or shiny objects, they're still promising, "soon," while apologizing to their kids, "Sorry, we can't afford it." Of course, StoryAthletes know… Money isn't the foundation of legacy. You can ask our ImpactClub® cofounders. Collectively, they have led local movements that have donated more than $2mil to local charities.

Everybody wants to enjoy superior health and mental fitness, to be able to execute at max productivity. They want to feel good about themselves. They don't want to be ashamed, when they look in the mirror. They want to inspire their kids to live a healthy life. They want to operate in *pure* flow state, where an hour passes by in 10 minutes. And, in that hour, they get more done than a normal person does all day. (In this place of extreme focus, due to *having* superior fitness of mind and body, resulting in Peak Energy, is how the best entrepreneurs are able to build a business and income in just weeks, or months vs. years or decades.)

Everybody wants to have the power to persuade and influence, to be able to inspire people with their words. The true currency of our society is not money, but stories. Stories are what create leaders. *Words* have the power to destroy. And the power to heal. Words can start wars. Or end wars. They have the power to build a person up. Or tear a person down. They can be used to inspire. *Or* to deliver the deepest cut. As parents, the greatest gift we can pass to our children is the power to be a *storyteller*. (When you and I die, I can assure you, our kids won't long for our material possessions. They will wish they could read the stories of our life; about the lessons we learned, the struggles we experienced, and the love we shared. I know, because I wish I could read my parents' stories. Except, they didn't write any.)

Everybody wants to travel and adventure to the most exotic locations with people they genuinely love. They want to attend masterminds. And experience growth with partners and friends who finally get and understand their ambition. From the Cliffs of Cabo to the mountain tops of Lake Tahoe. StoryAthletes have stayed in many of the nicest 25,000 sq.ft. homes. And twice each year, we gather at Live Events, in some of the most amazing places on earth to share our greatest breakthroughs; across mind, body, business, and relationships.

(But more importantly, to *hug* our best friends)

PARTNER:
WHAT DOES IT MEAN?

I suppose it means something different to everyone.

To Sloper and I, though, it means: we will bleed for you. Bleed for each other. Go to the end of the earth to ensure we can be counted on. Depended on. There is nothing worse to realize, when you're in the fight, and struggling, that you don't have a team of brothers you can count on.

A true Partner exhibits three behaviors:

1 - LOVE

If this makes you uncomfortable to admit, or to believe, that you could say to someone, "I love you, brother." And actually, mean it. Then I would question your ability to be a good partner. I'm not saying we "love each other" right off the bat. Take Mike Turner, for example, our ImpactClub® Boise cofounder. The first time I met Mike, I could barely stand him. He invaded my space. He was a close talker. And talked so much with his hands, it distracted the hell out of me. Today, I love Mike. I love Wayne. I love Melissa. I love Ron. I love Remy. I love Bob Grand and Eric Verdi. And so many others. We're all broken toys. And misfits. Sloper was once my customer. Now he is my family. Inside this Community, if you need something, you have an army of people to turn to. We love each other. We support each other. Through thick and thin, we fight together.

2 - COMMITMENT

We don't take this word lightly. And we don't take it lightly, because our commitments are to the people we love. When you're part of a Community, it's no longer *just* about you. When you have a family, it's no longer *just* about you. Further, this is about your Character. People make promises and commitments all the time, then break them, then sadly, don't think anything of it. This is why, in most cases, their lives don't work. They're not making the income they want. They don't have the body or mind they want. They don't have the time-freedom they want. They don't have the energy levels they want. They don't have the financial security they want. They struggle to be present in the moment. Hardly anything ever goes their way. This is because, in the words of Vince Lombardi, "Once someone learns to quit, quitting becomes the habit." In our world, quitters are the worst kind of people. Because those who quit, only care about themselves. Every time you quit on yourself, though, your teammates, partners, family members; spouse, kids, etc., are the ones who pay the price for your weakness. A commitment isn't about making a promise. A commitment is about proving the integrity of your Character, which becomes your Reputation. The greatest compliment any of us can receive, is to *kn-ooow* we can be counted on. We may not always win, but together, we'll never quit fighting. Life and business get easier, a lot easier, once you have teammates that have your back.

A side note about the importance of REPUTATION: Warren Buffett once said, "If you cost me money, I will be forgiving. If you cost me even a shred of my reputation, I will be ruthless." He did not say, "mad or angry." He said *"Ruthless!"* Why is this so important?

Because most people underestimate *just how much* our reputation (or lack of reputation) *rules our life* without us even knowing it. You get stereotyped *based on* your reputation. In other words, your reputation precedes you. It's how others judge you, *before* they know you.

Reputation is an unspoken language. In its purest and most powerful form, it's a language based entirely on sights and beliefs. It dictates how people perceive you. Whether you can be trusted (think of how politicians are perceived – can they be trusted?) Your reputation dictates your power, your influence, your authority; even to the degree others respect you. It's not until you understand how reputation works, that you can master it. <u>Take two real estate investors, for example. Real estate investing, by the way, is a Negative Reputation industry. Meaning, you are hated before you arrive. Distrusted before you speak a word. This Negative Reputation is due to the stereotype that homeowners have made, about investors, based on their experience with the typical wholesaler. "This motherfucker," they say, "Is trying to steal my property." Now, put both of them side-by-side. Except, one investor has successfully launched an ImpactClub® in his community that has donated more than $200K to local non-profits.</u> **Who wins?** The real estate investor with the Reputation of a real estate investor? Or the real estate investor with the Reputation of a Philanthropist, and *that* of a Community Leader? Later in this invitation, I will speak to the importance of storytelling to 1) *escape* Negative Reputation, but also 2) to create and *control* your OPN: Own Personal Narrative.

(Dan Kennedy, the famed direct-response marketer, and coach to many millionaire entrepreneurs, once said, "What you will be paid for, especially over time… more than for your know-how, more than for your service or work, more than for your results, more than anything… is your Reputation." So, why is it that so few entrepreneurs take the time to deliberately craft their Reputation, based on universally known *symbols* of trust, respect, and power?)

3 – EMPATHY

```
There are going to be times when you "can't go." There are going
to be times when things happen in your life, that take
precedence. No matter how much we want to be there for our
teammates, for our Partners, we just can't. This is not a
problem. We understand. Love and commitment to a teammate, who
knows your Character, because you have proven it, month after
month, for years, is never questioned in those times of need. A
commitment broken due to circumstance is not a loss or weakening
of reputation. Shit happens. Life happens. We understand. We may
be there ourselves one day. So, just know: Your teammates, for
whatever kind of support you need, are just a text or phone call
away. Empathy is about listening and understanding. Not
intolerance or judgement.
```

<u>Note:</u> Our community, StoryAthlete, has ripped no less than a dozen people from the brink of suicide back into the fire of life. Scott Mendell has openly told his story. He wrestled with the demon of death. He lost the desire to live. He gained a ton of weight. He sunk into

depression. He hid from the world. None of us judged him as weak. Just the opposite. We chose to battle alongside of him. Our Heroic Self leading by example, to re-inspire his. <u>Since then, Scott has lost 80-pounds. And mentally, reignited his passion to serve others. He is alive. Now, the leader of team #NeverQuit.</u> And anytime someone mentions serious depression, I connect them to Scott. He knows that enemy. And he knows how to defeat it.

MIND.

BODY.

BUSINESS.

RELATIONSHIPS.

The mission we have for each Partner inside of StoryAthlete: Each day, we become hard(er) to kill mentally, physically, financially, so that we may be "the Rock" to the relationships in our life.

To achieve this mission, requires that we do what is necessary. We succeed because we don't allow each other to slack.

Our commitment:

IT TAKES A FRIEND
...to call you on your shit.

A good friend, partner, doesn't care if they offend you. Their intent is not to hurt, but to intervene.

We thrive, or fail, based on the collective. Meaning, we either win together. Or we lose together. My business is your business. Your business is my business. My fitness is your fitness. Your fitness is my fitness. My mindset is your mindset. Your mindset is my mindset. <u>As a collective organism, as a Community seeking new discoveries, breakthroughs and innovations, we benefit, or pay the price, based on the strongest and weakest links in the system. If you're the weakest link, in any area, you become a non-contributing threat to the success of all.</u>

IN MIND – Let's start with your nutrition. For the person wanting to be an elite entrepreneur, our brain is our most prized tool. It should be protected. It should be nourished. What is your morning productivity habits? How many book pages are you processing each day? What is your organizational system to recall data? What mental models have you created to quickly solve complex problems? Is your decision-making governed by First Principles? What is your refined process to create Assets? What percentage of your day is committed to Asset-creation? How many Assets have you created in the last month? How are you documenting your experiences? Are you turning your *stories* into books? Since writing is the highest form of thinking, *how much* writing are you doing? <u>Back to your nutrition. If you shovel "heaps of coal" into your body, as your primary source of nutrition, then all this stuff that is already difficult, becomes 10X more difficult because your brain is running on sludge</u>. Your brain is no different than the engine in your car. If you put sugar in the tank, it really fucks it up. So, if one is serious about operating as an elite entrepreneur, to become a valuable Partner in the Community, *how* have they optimized their energy protocol?

> **A tired brain doesn't give a shit about anything**. It doesn't care about your desire to serve. The promises you made to yourself. Nor the commitments you made to others. It will sabotage every best intention you have. The Lesser Self is driven by weak-brain decisions.
>
>> Now, if you don't have good answers to those questions above - why not? You said you wanted to be elite. You said you wanted to be a good partner. The elite entrepreneur trains his brain as an elite Athlete trains their body. Busyness cannot be confused for productivity. Activities cannot be confused for Assets. And mental fatigue, due to poor mental habits, cannot be the excuse for poor execution. <u>The fitness of our Mind is what separates us from the masses of wannabees</u>.
>>
>>> Note: The library of information that I have both purchased and created, through the books I bought, the mentors I've hired, and stories I have penned, is more valuable than any college education. As a parent, it is my duty to pass the expensive lessons I have paid for, and suffered from making, as well as the discoveries I have made, and the winnings I have gained because of them, onto my kids. The content I create is for them. <u>If I asked to see your library of intellectual property (IP), that you have created for your kids, how big would it be?</u>

IN BODY – Let's start with your physical fitness. I used to be 40-pounds heavier. I thought I was a high-performing entrepreneur. Then I lost that forty-pounds. What that did for my energy levels, brain performance, etc., by putting "Fat Ryan" back in the box," changed everything. The Body is the vehicle for the mind. It is the *chassis*. The engine. Through fitness + nutrition (achieved through GRIT + FUEL) we extend the battery-life of our brain. Think about your laptop. <u>What happens to the performance of your computer, when the battery reaches that critically low 5-10% threshold? Exactly. Performance drags to a halt</u>. Processing speed is torturous slow. Some computers have a battery-life of 10-hours. Others have a battery life of 2 hours. This is true for entrepreneurs, too. Some can knock out 10-hour days of uninterrupted Deep Work. Others get distracted constantly, barely knocking out 2 hours each day. One is proficient at building companies. The other only dreams about building those same companies. <u>But struggles to build them, and gets frustrated by their slow progress, because their battery life each day is 500% less.</u> The elite entrepreneur doesn't train their Body because they love fitness. They train their Body, getting into Peak physical fitness, resulting in Peak Energy, to extend the battery-life of their Mind.

> **This isn't solely about extending battery-life though**. This is about living a life of demonstration for our kids. Here are two startling facts: One in six Americans are prescribed an anti-depressant. Anti-depressant usage correlate tightly to the rise in obesity rates. It is damn hard to feel good about yourself, when you are fat. It is damn hard to feel strong, when you are winded by walking up the stairs. It is damn hard to say yes, to doing hard things, when hard things, physically, cause you extreme pain. We all know the importance of getting in good physical shape, for our health. Yet, six out of every 10 in our society are obese.
>
>> <u>This is about inspiring our kids, and loved ones, through our own committed actions</u>. After I lost 40-pounds, I inspired my brother to join me in living the Challenged-based life. In six months, he quickly lost 40-Pounds, too. His wife, Christi, in that same span, lost more than 30-pounds and 25- total inches. Men want their wives to look hot and attractive, and to be physically fit, but then so many don't hold themselves to that same standard. Every parent wants their kids to be physically fit, and healthy, to get outside and play. But then, by their actions, they condone a life of stagnation, eating crap food, and are overweight themselves. No bullshit. Go look in the mirror. How proud of yourself are you, for the body you have cultivated? *(I wasn't proud of mine)*
>>
>>> **Heroic Self vs. Lesser Self**. If we're going to claim to be leaders, then we must lead by example. An overweight child (son or daughter) will be forced to live an infinitely harder life. Being picked on. Being bullied. Low self-confidence and self-esteem. Less attractive to the opposite sex. Developing eating disorders. Starts using their weight, and jokes about it, as the foundation of self-depreciating humor. Depression, suicide. These are soaring epidemics for teenagers. They are soaring epidemics that have everything to do with low self-esteem. Low self-worth. And no inner strength. <u>I'm a pretty confident person, and yet, even I, when I looked in the mirror at "Fat Ryan," my Lesser Self, wished that motherfucker would die</u>. I can only imagine what a kid must go through, socially, mentally, who is considerably overweight. So, the question is: Are you leading by example? <u>Are you, through your own actions, inspiring your kids to know what fitness looks like? This is about the mental health of your family!</u>

IN BUSINESS – Let's start with your created Assets. There are two driving factors that explain why most people get into business. 1) Time-freedom. And 2) financial security. And the reason that most entrepreneurs never achieve either one, is because they fail to create Assets to get leveraged. So, year after year, they trade time for money. If they stop working, they stop getting paid. Assets are like oil wells. You build them once. They pump and pump, for you, forever. <u>There are three (3) phases to business growth: Acquisition. Retention. Ascension. Most businesses starve because they don't have good marketing system(s) in place. Or, because they don't have good Ops and automations in place. Or they don't have a good ascension path in place. This chain of dominos starts with</u>: What is the message that differentiates you? What stories have you told and retold to create and control the Narrative (leading to the Reputation) of your product, service, Character, or documented approach? If we simplify the acquisition phase into its simplest form, you get: <u>Traffic + Offer = Money</u>. There are only two components. So, what is the Offer that you have crafted that 1) creates demand for your business, 2) differentiates you from competitors, 3) identifies and speaks only to your *defined* target avatar, and 4) introduces a new path forward, both superior and different than the previous or alternative options? <u>Now, to sell this Offer, what sales process have you designed to maximize conversion rate? Then what funnel structure have you built, with good copywriting, to automate the sales process?</u> Then, what traffic sources have you tested to know whether your Offer is capable of acquiring new customers, users, clients, within KPI (key performance indicator) metrics? <u>Have you done this?</u> And if the CPA (cost per acquisition) is outside of your KPI, have you installed Risk Mitigation Protocols, or the "Mass Market to Niche, Niche to Mass Market" concept on the Offer, to increase the AOV (average order value) and LCV (lifetime customer value), thus, allowing you to increase the allowable CPA that you can afford to spend on the front-end? **At this point, most entrepreneurs, as they look objectively at their business, don't have a clue what I'm even saying here. Which means they have no *real* client-acquisition Assets in their business**. Which means, they are stuck on the treadmill. Like that little rat, on a hamster wheel, running and running, hoping to one day get off, but have no clear path of *how* to actually make that happen. Two years pass. Five years pass. A decade passes…

> **We create Assets because we want a great life, provided by a business that serves us**. Everybody is familiar with ROI: Return on investment. But how many think in terms of ROT: Return on time? I can tell you, not many! If they did, they would prioritize Asset creation. If I spend an hour right now, creating an Asset, how many hundreds of times can I leverage that hour into the future?
>
>> Most people think making money is hard. It's only hard, though, because of how most people are taught to make money. The hard way. "Work hard. Grind for years. Put in more hours." This leads to the typical worker-bee mentality. That is how the barista at Starbucks works. "Hi-ho, Hi-ho, off to work I go." It's not how the elite entrepreneur should build their business, though, for scale or profitability. <u>There are five phases to building high-value assets in your business. Phase 1 – Message. Phase 2 –</u>

> Offer. Phase 3 - Writing the copy. Phase 4 - Funnels and traffic. Phase 5 - Ops and automations.
>
> This five-phase protocol is like gravity. If you try to defy it, you die. Your Assets never get optimized. If you execute the protocol though, then time-freedom and financial security are the resulting benefits. For the Asset Control Specialist class, for example, which is but a clone of the Class Acquisition Funnel template that I designed, we spend tens of thousands every month, in paid ads, to acquire new customers. I crafted the Message once. I built the Offer once. I wrote the copy once. I built the funnel and designed the traffic strategy once. Sloper and I delivered the class once; recorded all the content and put it in a membership site. From there, Ops were put in place and automations built around it. In the first 60-days, that newly created Asset did more than $50K in sales and, week to week, requires only 15 minutes of my time each Saturday morning to fulfill.
>
>> **A $600K savings**: When we launched ImpactClub®, we had no clue what Operations even were. All of a sudden, we had all of this work that needed to get done, and no more time in our schedules to do the work. So, we started hiring. We had 13 in-house employees. We also had a team of 30+ freelancers. My monthly overhead ballooned real-quick to over $50K per month. Today, with just one employee, thanks to Ops and Automations, we get more work done than when we had thirteen.
>>
>>> Note: For every part of this 5-Phase process, to build high-value Assets in your business, we have you covered. Our business should exist to serve us. Not to enslave us. It's not hard to make a couple hundred thousand per year, completely automated. Inside of your business, have you built the *Assets* to enable this?

IN RELATIONSHIPS – Let's start with your *path to* happiness. On every airplane, they say, "Put on. Secure your mask first." There is a reason for this. Before you can save others, you must save yourself. **If you're unhappy with you; your weight, your confidence, your status as a provider, your energy levels, etc., then you will forever struggle to create powerful relationships**. You can't pour into others from an empty cup. The person dissatisfied with themselves, and their strength across Mind, Body, Business, Relationships, operates from a place of blame and scarcity. Everything is someone else's fault. Jealousy and envy are driving forces of unhappiness for this person. They are stressed. Financially, they *perpetually* compare their position in life to others. They feel small. Like they're not enough. They feel insignificant. They feel like they're not serving their spouse or family at the highest level. They struggle to love themselves. Hence, the reason that one out of every six

Americans is prescribed to some kind of anti-depressant. **What happens though, when the Lesser Self is defeated by the Heroic Self?** You properly condition your Mind, to powerfully solve problems, by creating productivity habits, focused on Asset-creation, *spurred* from mental models. What happens when you properly train your body (GRIT + FUEL) to achieve Peak Energy, to extend the batter-life of your brain? Peak Energy is that rare elixir that can't be understood until it is achieved. Before you had sex, someone may have tried to describe it to you. But you had to experience it to *really* understand it. What happens when the Heroic Self triples down on creating on Assets, that get leveraged to maximize ROT: return on time, which in turn, propels ROI: return on investment? Exactly, time-freedom and financial security move through the roof. What happens when, collectively, across these different dimensions, Mind, Body, Business, get transformed, making us hard(er) to kill mentally, physically, financially? The end result is self-love. Confidence. No financial stress. Happiness. Now, our cup is full, and we can pour into others…

> **My kids thought I didn't want to play with them.** Everything I have talked about above, across Mind, Body, and Business, and the frustration and failures at each stage, stem from my own experiences. As mentioned, I used to be super fat. "Fat Ryan" got up early, poured everything he had into business. Financially, he was a success. But to his kids, he was an utter failure. All the time, my kids would ask, "Dad, want to play catch?" "Dad, want to play soccer?" "Dad, want to jump on the trampoline?" Each time, I would say, No, no, no. Not because I didn't want to. But because I knew each of those activities would have me physically exhausted and panting for air in a matter of minutes. When I ran, or attempted to jump, I could feel my fat ass wiggle and shake. I told my kids, "No, no, no" because I was *only* thinking about me. Protecting my own insecurities. Truth is, I was fucking ashamed and embarrassed by how out of shape I had let myself become. Then one day, I heard something that broke my heart. Zoey said to Jackson, "Go ask Dad if he wants to play with us." Jackson said, reflexively, "He doesn't want to play with us. Why even bother to ask?" As a father, that crushed me. He was right, though. I had said "No, no, no" so many times. That is the narrative that I instilled him. "Dad doesn't like to play with us." So, I committed to change. I dropped 40-pounds. Family fitness is now part of our bonding. A few months later, I asked Jackson, "Which Dad do you like better: That old Fat Dad or this New Dad?" He said, "This new Dad." I said "Me, too." Write this down: Those who suffer together, bond together. Through fitness, and by doing grueling workouts together, as parents, we have the ability to bond deeply with our kids. So many life lessons, about success and failure, are taught through the struggle to keep going. Until I changed my relationship with fitness, I couldn't change the relationships with my kids.
>
> > **My wife got the worst part of me.** As a provider, I used my business success as the justification for why I was never present in the moment. "I have to meet this deadline." "I have to return this email." "I have to get *this* to employee X, Y or Z." I would always be looking at my phone. I would always come in late to dinner. I would always be working on

Saturdays and Sundays. And since I got up at 4:30am every morning, by 6:30pm, right after dinner, I was beat. I'd crash on the couch and fall asleep. And if I didn't, then I was just a dick to be around. I was tired. I was irritable. I thought this was normal. But then, when I lost that 40-pounds, and changed how I fueled my body. My energy levels went through the roof. I still got up at 4:30am. But I wasn't even tired until 9pm. And because my mind was so much clearer, more productive, I got 2-5X more work done each day. This led to me working less hours. I didn't need to work so many hours. I stopped working Saturdays and Sundays. I came in early for dinner. I had an abundance of energy. I wasn't lethargic anymore. I wasn't tired. I wasn't that "same irritable dick" that neglected the needs of his wife. <u>This is when I realized, my wife, for years, had been getting the leftovers of me. Whatever I had left in the tank, at the end of the day, which was never much, that is what she got from me. I was a shitty husband. I was a shitty partner. I was too fat to even make love well. And half the time, I said "no" to her because I was tired, exhausted, and just wanted to sleep</u>. It wasn't until I changed my relationship with nutrition, to achieve Peak Energy, that I could change my relationship with my wife. A tired brain, as mentioned, doesn't have the ability to care about anything but itself.

Personal vs. Business Relationships. I want to share a secret with you. We all agree relationships are the cornerstone of life. Without strong relationships, that bring connection and purpose, as entrepreneurs, what is the point of our sacrifice? We take risks to create a better life for those that count on us, depend on us. Our families. But also, we take risks and reveal ourselves, becoming open and vulnerable, often to complete strangers to give meaning to the work we do, as we connect with the people we serve; customers, clients, members. <u>I am often asked, "How or where do you invest your money?" What happens next is, I usually get a strange, sort of weird look from the person who just heard my answer</u>. When you look at their face, it's apparent, they're confused. You can see the wheels turning in their head. Their eyes sort of squint up. Their head cocks one way. Their brows start to twitch. Clearly, these folks just heard something they didn't quite understand. To them, my answer, what they heard, was like seeing an alien from a distant galaxy. To which, they always ask: "You invest in what?!" I repeat, "I invest in people," I say. "I invest in the relationship with my audience." These are the people who read my books, listen to my podcasts, watch my videos, consume my morning emails, etc. <u>It's called the Reader-Writer-Relationship. This is what turns a complete stranger, a new customer, who just discovered me for the first time, into a life-long follower of my work</u>.

Financial Security. Make sure to write this down. To make money, the formula (as discussed) is simple: Traffic + Offer = Money. But money comes and goes. Lots of people make a lot of money, but then spend it, so they must continually hunt it. Financial Security is quite different. <u>Financial Security means you have a replenishing source of funds. How do you achieve this? Write this down: Traffic + Offer + Storytelling = Financial Security</u>. Because, through storytelling, specifically, Sitcom-based content, you build the Reader-Writer Relationship to create an audience that knows, likes and trusts you. Every time you write an email, they want to read it. Every time you release a new video, they want to watch it. Every time you post a new podcast, they want to listen to it. <u>This connection to your message (rooted in your values, beliefs, and convictions) is what compels your audience, to be eager and willing to buy whatever Offer you put in front of them next</u>. No different than how a music lover buys all the music of his or her favorite band. Or how a book reader buys every new release from his or her favorite author. This should happen in your business, too. People often ask how we achieve, inside of our companies, lifetime customer values that range up to $50-75K. This is how. Story + Athlete. Story = The Sport. Athlete = Elite performance. We use storytelling to create the Reader-Writer Relationship.

> **Think about *that* in investment terms**. It only cost me $150 to acquire that customer. An acquisition cost that I only had to pay once. Now, ten years later, that customer, like Eric Verdi, is still a customer of mine and has paid me over $50K. What is that ROI: return on investment? <u>Can you get that kind of return in the Stock Market or even by investing in real estate?</u> This is why I invest my money into building a connected audience.

The relationship with myself. Listen closely to this. I even changed the *rhythm* of the indenting-pattern (for this section) to make sure this paragraph stuck out. In my heart of hearts, back in 2018, I knew I had to confront myself. I was doing much of the business stuff right. Business growth and my income proved that. But I was failing in too many other parts of my life. I was letting down my wife. I was failing my kids. I had no time. I had no energy. I was fat. I hated how I looked in the mirror and on camera. I was embarrassed by how out of shape I had allowed myself to become. My singular focus on business, led to an unhappy life. About this time, back in 2018, I remembered a piece written by Steve Jobs, supposedly, from his hospital bed, as he was days away from dying from pancreatic cancer. "<u>I reached the pinnacle of success in the business world</u>," he wrote. "In others' eyes, my life is an epitome of success. However, aside from work, I HAVE LITTLE JOY. In the end, wealth is only a fact of life that I am accustomed to. At this moment, lying on the sick bed and recalling my whole life, I realize that all the recognition and wealth that I took so much pride in, have paled and become meaningless in the face of impending death." I wasn't dying. But this is how I felt, too. I HAD LITTLE JOY. I had built a 7-figure business in 12-months, and yet despite this success, I had no joy. I had regret. My life and relationships were literally falling apart around me.

Which gets to a recent post by Sean Whalen, who referenced that same *Jobs* quote. In his post, Sean wrote "We spend the majority of our adult life accumulating assets that are meaningless in that moment. We spend years building empires when the people living in the empires don't even know us. We swing dicks to compare balance sheets and net worth, when those most precious to us understand PRESENCE & EXPERIENCE, not EBIDA: earnings before interest, depreciation and amortization. Fathom having Steve Jobs here today. Sitting in our boardrooms. I wonder what he'd say. I wonder if he'd focus on our bottom-line or tell us to take that trip." Sean went on to write, "The game of money is a simple one. X's & O's. Add value, add wealth. That's the simple shit. The game of LIFE. That is the true genius. That is the real game to figure out and play." Followed, by saying, "I'd like to consider myself a smart fella. I've made millions. I've lost millions. I've made them again. That game is easy. I'd like to think that I'm smart enough to not only hear the words of a dying billionaire, but to LIVE them. So, when I'm lying on my deathbed I can simply smile at my independently wealthy and in need of nothing posterity and say, "what a fucking ride" then cross over and tell Steve, I heard you, and I did it all bro." *My own epiphany?...*

I spent a lot of years allowing my Business to become my life, and frankly, it nearly destroyed my family. So now, a much better approach I have found, is to turn my Life into my business.

Re-read those two sentences by Sean:

1) The game of money is a simple one. X's & O's. Add value, add wealth. That's the simple shit.

2) The game of LIFE. That is the true genius. That is the real game to figure out and play.

I came to this same realization, too, as my financially-successful-life started to collapse in around me.

The game of money, Sean is right.

That's the simple shit.

The game of LIFE? That is the true genius. And the most challenging *Game* to figure out and master.

Mind.

Body.

Business.

Relationships.

BALANCE vs. INTEGRATION

This isn't about work-life balance. This is about Work-Life Integration, where literally, your fitness becomes part of your business. Where creating a regimen for your mind, literally, becomes part of your business.

Where being present with your kids and spouse, becomes part of your business. Where attending masterminds, with some of your best friends and business partners, becomes part of your business.

Where impacting your community, donating tens-of-thousands, even hundreds-of-thousands to local charities, becomes part of your business.

Where documenting the lessons you've learned into stories, literally, become part of the business.

If you want to get paid to read books, great. If you want to get paid to lose weight or to run in a Spartan race, great. If you want to get paid to invest in real estate, and because you inspired others, great.

The Masses vs. The 5%

For people like us, the 5% most ambitious, work-life balance DOES. NOT. WORK! Work-life balance is a failed model. People like me, I've discovered, are not good at balance. We are extremists. This is what makes us great. We push. And charge! And are willing to sacrifice. We don't stop. We don't quit. The only speed we know, is *go*, run *faster*, achieve more…

<u>As soon as we achieve one benchmark, we notoriously move the needle, higher and higher, effectively causing us to start over</u>. This is why, when we make that promise to our kids or spouse, "It's not always going to be like this." "One day, it will be different." Meaning, we made the money. We built the business. We have achieved financial security. That promise - *is a LIE*. Because it's "Always going to be this way," precisely because *achieving* is who we are.

We don't know how to play the game to "good-enough," then just leave it alone. We play until we achieve or win. Then we immediately set our sight on the horizon, as we aim to level up.

The 5% most ambitious are Extremists.

They go "All in."

We don't know any other way to play.

So, knowing this about myself, I knew I had to design a business where my *LIFE* became the business. That way, when I went all *extremist*, I became healthier, more fit, a better father and husband…

Hard(er) to kill; mentally, physically, financially.

The optimization *of me*.

The *optimization* of my family…

<u>Documenting on the journey; my challenges and struggles, hardships, along with my successes, adventures, and transformations</u>. My product *became* Work-Life Integration. How do I show others that are suffering my *same* extremist, destructive behaviors, how to harness their ambition? – how to put it to work, to optimize themselves, their family, where the harder they work *in* their business, which is now their *Life*, the more optimized they become as a parent, spouse, community leader…

And, as someone who *inspires* others.

StoryAthlete
Get Paid To Become Your Best Self!

Most people, if we're being honest, think this is all bullshit. At this point, they are saying, *"Yeah, sounds amazing."* If only *"that"* could be true. Get paid to become my best self. Get paid to focus on me. Get paid to workout. Get paid to build my family. Get paid to read books. Get paid to invest in real estate. Get paid to *better myself* as a parent, as a spouse.

Get *paid* to write stories…

> TRUTH #1 – Inspiring others is a real profession (Transformation drives demand)
>
> TRUTH #2 – Leverage partners (Business vs. Income)
>
> TRUTH #3 – Proven frameworks (Combat Failure & Disease)
>
> TRUTH #4 – Sacrifice is required (CRISPR: to replace defective "gene sequences")
>
> TRUTH #5 – Harness compounding (The 8th wonder of the world)

Let's start with #1…

TRUTH #1
Inspiring Others Is a Real Profession

I don't want to overcomplicate this, because it is a *truth* that is simple to understand. If I lose 40-pounds, and someone else needs to lose 40-pounds, because I have done it already, this is what they ask, *"How did you do it?"*

This is called *demand*.

The foundation of business, for any kind of business, is the process of creating demand for your product or service. How you create demand is by achieving a Before & After transformation.

I used to be Fat – "Fat Ryan."

Then I lost 40-pounds – "Fat Ryan" is gone.

Before. After.

I could show you those photos, and you would say, "Damn, you look way better than "Fat Ryan" did. And because I really did lose 40-pounds, tons of people asked me that exact question…

"How did you do it?"

"What is your secret?"

I got asked that question so many times, I partnered with CJ Thomas, StoryAthlete's personal trainer, to create the GRIT program. So now, together, through GRIT, we run a kind of fitness business.

I have no business being in the fitness industry. But my transformation, through an insanely simple protocol, created *demand* for the same process that transformed me, to transform others.

NOW STOP…

AND UNDERSTAND…

REALLY INTERNALIZE…

<u>WHAT</u> I JUST

SAID.

Transformation **Drives Demand**

<u>I see so many good people struggle in business, and struggle to get customers and clients, and thus struggle to make the income they want</u>, because they didn't stop long enough to understand this *simple* truth.

So please, stop, and understand, this is the response every entrepreneur should aim to create inside of people.

"How did you do it?"

"What is your secret?"

As a business, Sloper and I never really intended to teach the *Asset Control Specialist* model. But, because so many kept *failing* in their quest to a become full-time real estate investor, and we kept succeeding, one by one, for years, before we created the ACS class, people asked us…

"How do you do it?"

"What is your secret?"

So, finally, in the same spirit of how GRIT was founded, we launched the ACS class because there was *demand*. The first class started June 10th, 2020. In the first two months alone, more than $50K was collected in registrations, from 400+ people that wanted to learn our model.

Everybody says, "Making money is hard."

No, it isn't hard.

So here, and now, let me reveal to you the formula for turning any passion into your business. It's quite simple:

Step 1 – Do Hard Shit

You have to be willing to do hard shit. Because by doing the kind of hard shit that others would like to do. But - insert excuses: Not enough time. Not enough money. Not convenient enough. Not smart enough. Not experienced enough. Too hard. Etc. This is what gets you the *Transformative Result* that other people want, but can't have, because they weren't willing to do what you did…

To lose 40-pounds, I did two things.

I cut sugar.

And I executed a daily *GRIT* workout that took 12-minutes, to as much as 20-minutes.

"What is your secret?"

That is my secret. And yet, despite the simplicity of that prescription. Guaranteed to bring transformation. Hardly anyone, who asked me, "How did you do it?" actually did it, as I instructed…

Step 2 – Stick With It

You guessed it, they all quit within day or a week, because it was "too hard" to give up "sugar." Not to mention, 12-min of exercise each day, apparently, is just "too hard" for people to sustain their commitment to.

This is why fat people stay fat.

This is why most people who buy courses, too, never execute or implement the information they purchased.

Lots of people start.

Very few people finish!

Most just bounce from one "shiny object" to the next. One RE investing course to the next. From one diet fad to the next. Each time, searching for a simpler, faster, easier way to get the result…

Step 3 – Get a Result

Getting the Transformative Result is one of the *simplest* things on earth to achieve. "Everything you want in life can be had, *if*…you just stop quitting on yourself." Those 15-words are the secret.

Everyone else will stop, give up, and quit.

You?

Don't quit.

This is how you achieve the Transformative Result that others wish they could get, have, experience, **but can't**, because they chose *not* to do what you did, as you sustained your commitment…

Lots of people start on the path to becoming a full-time real estate investor, but then quit. So, they don't get to experience the lifestyle, freedom, or financial certainty, that we do.

Lots of people start on the path to becoming healthier, more physically fit, but then quit. So, they don't get to experience the Peak Energy, clarity of mind, or productivity, that we do.

Lots of people start on the path to building a true marketing system for their business, but then quit. So, they don't get to enjoy the steady stream of new clients, and deal flow, that we do.

Lots of people start on the path to becoming a great storyteller, but then quit. So, they don't get to experience the power of connection, influence, or the ability to inspire others, like we do.

We start.

We stick with it.

***We* get the Transformative Result!**

And because of that personal transformation, because we chose to do the hard shit, to change and *transform* our lives. Our financial future. Our health and well-being. To impact our Communities. To build a stronger family. Again, and again, StoryAthletes are asked…

"How did you do it."

"What's your secret?"

NOW STOP, AND UNDERSTAND…

REALLY INTERNALIZE…

WHAT I JUST

SAID.

Understanding this concept, deeper than surface level, could be worth more than a million dollars to you.

It's been worth many millions of dollars to me.

And, it's so simple.

When people ask you, "How did you do it?" "What is your secret?" They are begging you, you as their guide, to point them in the direction that you moved, so they too, can get the same result.

Do you understand the *power position* this puts you in?

Now, let's *market* your transformation!

 TRUTH #1 – (Part 2) Transformation drives demand

Do you understand what this does for your *ability* to be seen as "a Someone" to others, wanting your help?

Maybe you've never thought of yourself as an Influencer before.

Maybe you never thought you could build a large audience, interested in what you have to say.

Maybe you've never thought of yourself as a *Storyteller*, that people would want to listen to.

Maybe you're *still* uncertain of how you'd monetize such an audience, even if you had an audience.

 TRUTH #1 – (Part 1) Inspiring others is a real profession.

Monetization is easy.

You say, "Here's the link…"

As a Partner of StoryAthlete, where StoryAthlete becomes your Community, is part of your business, would it be hard to share a link to a resource that has profoundly impacted your life?

Mind, Body, Business, Relationships…

TRUTH #2
Leverage Partners (Business vs. Income)

For too long, I didn't understand the power of this concept. I foolishly believed that if I was compensated in anyway, by a company, because I recommended their product or service, then my recommendation would be perceived to be *in*authentic. And I would be judged, a scammer.

This is such a stupid (limiting) belief.

Never in my life, have I, nor would I, ever recommend a product or service that I don't use, or hasn't significantly impacted my life. Take my copywriting peer, Sean Vosler. I deeply respect his work. He's poured his heart and soul into creating an incredible copywriting product.

I have bought it.

I use it. I reference it, frequently.

If I tell you, go here:
https://app.increase.academy/this-is-the-most-important-entrepreneur-skill

Or, to go here:
https://app.increase.academy/this-is-the-most-important-entrepreneur-skill?affiliate_id=2381450

Does it *really* make any difference?

Not really.

Except, that 2nd link is my partner link, where if you decide to purchase Sean's work, he'll pay me a commission. A commission, that if he had to *do* paid-advertising, he'd pay to Google or Facebook.

As Sean said to me, "I'd rather pay you, than Google or FB."

Recommending Sean's work is something I'm happy to do, because I haven't created a great copywriting product. He has.

People ask me all the time, what marketing software I use to build my funnels and run my business on. For a long time, I said ClickFunnels, and then sent people to the ClickFunnels homepage.

And, I got paid *nothing* for doing that.

Now.

I still say "ClickFunnels"

But I send them here:
https://www.clickfunnels.com/?cf_affiliate_id=620668

And because of that simple difference in the link, instead of making *nothing* from my authentic recommendation. This year, ClickFunnels will pay me north of $40K in partner revenue.

The best part?

Business vs. INCOME

To make that $40K in partner revenue, I didn't have to do a thing. That is the beauty. I'm not responsible for any customer service. No fulfillment. No customer onboarding. No product development. No team meetings. I didn't have to hire. I didn't have to build any funnels...

Russell Brunson built the funnels. He's a phenomenal copywriter, and his 500+ employees, are responsible for all the customer service, delivery of the product, and building the business.

I just *shared* a partner link.

And for my authentic recommendation, I get 40% of the ongoing revenue for that customer sale.

That's MRR: Monthly Recurring Revenue.

I don't own the business.

I *own* the income.

And guess what? I can create as many of these recurring revenue streams as I want, as I partner with different companies and recommend their product or service, because they impacted my life.

Everybody says, "Making money is hard."

No, it isn't hard.

So here, let me reveal to you the 2nd set of steps to create an Income without the headaches of the business:

Step 1 – Design Your Transformation

Remember, transformation *drives* demand.

"How did you do it."

"What's your secret?"

And, when people ask that question, you say, "Here's how. Go here…"

So, be smart.

Design your ideal life, so that as you work hard to achieve your transformation, you not only transform your life, yourself, and your family, but you are creating *demand* for the path you walk.

From wanting to be a Real estate investor → To completing your first deal.

= People will ask, "What's your secret?"

= You will say, "Here's how I did it - *Go here…*"

= *Get Paid to Become Your Best Self*

From overweight & out-of-shape → To losing 40-pounds and being in the best shape of your life.

= People will ask, "What's your secret?"

= You will say, "Here's how I did it - *Go here…*"

= *Get Paid to Become Your Best Self*

From wanting to build a lucrative online business → To enjoying multiple streams of recurring revenue.

From wanting to be a more present parent → To working 50% few hours because of created assets.

From wanting to impact your community → To donating tens-of-thousands to local charities every quarter.

From living in a place of stress and depression → To living a life of extreme achievement.

From knowing you have a message inside of you → To actually publishing that message into a book.

<u>From starting and stopping → To starting and *finishing*</u>!

Step 1 – Do Hard Shit

Step 2 – Stick With It

Step 3 – Get The Result

People will ask, "What's your secret?"

= You will say, "Here's how I did it - *Go here…*"

= ***Get Paid to Become Your Best Self***

Obviously, I can't know what your *ideal* transformation looks like, as you design the path that your Character will travel. But I do know, this is how you turn your LIFE into your business.

And, in traveling your *designed* path, you create the reputation and narrative, in the mind of others, who want your same Transformative Result, that *you're* the person who has the answers.

How do you amplify this?

To *become* that person with the Empowering Reputation – that serves you…

Crafted Positioning…

Step 2 – Document The Journey

Part of your designed transformation is the *ability* to become a StoryAthlete. Story = the sport. Athlete = Elite performance. Writing is not hard. Writer's block is not real. You *just* document…

<u>Before. During. After.</u>

Before - *This* is the origin story.

Why do you want to change? This is the part of the story that reveals your motive. Your life isn't working. Your health is declining. Your financial future sucks. Or your income is good, but you have *no time* for your family. You're never present with your kids. Your spouse gets the worst of you. You haven't built any assets. You keep starting. Then stopping. You keep quitting on yourself. You keep promising a new life. You're sick of not living up to your potential. You're embarrassed as a financial provider. You're always tired. You lack energy. You're frustrated. You're distracted. You can't focus. <u>Life wasn't supposed to be this way. Then something happens. Enough is enough. Not for another minute. Not for another second can you tolerate your current situation</u>. You have experienced the *Turning Point*. The straw that broke the camel's back. You decide! Something must change! I must change it! And the motive is created.

In this "hole of Darkness" is where the vast majority of people live their life. As Henry David Thoreau put it, "The mass of men lead quiet lives of desperation. What is called *resignation* is confirmed desperation." In other words, they resign, quit, give up, because they are eager to make their suffering stop. If they can just stop wanting, they can be content with not having. In this same sentiment, <u>Benjamin Franklin observed, "Some people die at 25 but aren't buried until 75." Those people? They're still here. *Still* with us. Still alive. But they're not living. Not *truly* living. They stopped pursuing their potential. They accepted themselves as failures and quit</u>. The prevalence of this: "Hole of Darkness" "A life of quiet desperation" "Alive, but not really living" is confirmed by the fact that one in every six Americans is prescribed to some kind of anti-depressant. It seems - America, once a land of eternal optimism, by the millions, is losing hope.

Your journey can be a *Light* to those in the Dark. To some, frustration, overwhelm, depression, these are reasons to quit. To others, that frustration, challenge, and unhappiness, is a call to action. Some people hear this call, some people don't. Most don't. But StoryAthletes aren't most people. No matter how deep, or how dark that hole is, we hear the drum beat inside. To the last breath, *we fight*.

<u>During</u> – *This* is the struggle:

This is the hero's journey. This is the part of the story that reveals the pain, the agony, the sacrifice that our Character makes in order to achieve his objective. He's faced with hardships. Nothing goes his way. Luck is against him. He's out of his depths. He's scared. He's exhausted. He wants to quit. He wants to turn back. <u>The pain is such that he begs to return to his previous, ordinary life. But, something inside of him, his *why*, won't let him quit. He pushes ahead. He forges into the fray. He refuses to be defeated</u>. The entire time, though, the Lesser Self is trying to sabotage him. Turn back. Just stop. You don't need to do this. You've earned it. Take a break. Go back to your comfort zone. But, he doesn't. He is the 5%, not the 95%, who completes the Hero's Journey. To experience and achieve the transformative result. It wasn't easy. It was incredibly difficult and hard. But he did it. And he let others, by documenting his journey, telling his stories, to live vicariously through his struggle.

> **The Hero isn't the person who achieves the transformative result with ease.** The Hero is the person who struggles, almost failed, had every reason to quit and give up, but didn't. As a result, through perseverance, they achieved.
>
>> **The power of "the Struggle."** <u>This is where ALL the connection and inspiration live with the people who follow your journey and read your stories</u>. In the struggle is where they discover your courage, and mental toughness, by seeing your willingness to continue on. To keep fighting. Even when you don't want to. Even when the odds are stacked against you. And the fact that you don't quit, despite the mounting number of challenges, gives them hope that maybe they, too, can achieve what you are fighting to achieve.

After – *This* is the envy:

> **What's your secret?** This is the part where they want to be like you. Think like you. Operate like you. Think, Michael Jordan, "Be Like Mike." You and I may not be Jordan. But as the *Light* to those in the Dark, who we inspired and connected with, through our stories, we might as well be. The Reader-writer relationship is the *path* to rare kind of fame. It's not Hollywood fame. It's a 1,000 True Fans fame. To most people, you will be a nobody. But to those 1,000 True Fans, you are the person who changed, shifted, and altered the course of their life. This is how audiences are built. Not by the millions at a time. But one person at a time, as they say: "I like the way this guy thinks." Beliefs. Values. Convictions. "I like the way this guy plays." Hard work. Discipline. Mental toughness. "I like the way this guy operates." A person who doesn't quit. A person who achieves. "I – want to *be* like that." "I – want to *play* as he does." "I – want to *think* as he does." "I – want to *achieve* as he does." This is what compels a person to want to *continually* listen to your message. Read your stories.
>
>> **Don't be confused.** <u>Through the shared struggle, not the envy, is how you build your tribe</u>. Don't be afraid to be human. Failure is part of the journey. Don't be embarrassed by your starting point. Don't be humiliated because it

didn't or doesn't, come easy to you. Don't hide because you finished last. Or second to last. YOU become a hero, in the eyes of the people who read your stories, based on your effort and perseverance, not based on the place you finish. Talent can be wasted. Had work never is. Sacrifice never is. Becoming harder to kill; mentally, physically, financially, is a process.

Reaching our potential requires patience. Just accept the fact, it's not going to happen as fast we you thought. It's going to be harder than expected. It's going to cost 5X as much as anticipated. The solution to each of these is the 1% journey. Each day, put in the work. Each day, put in the focus. Each day, execute the next step. Day after day, continue to check that next box. Don't quit. Don't stop. Don't wish for it to be easier. Just focus on you becoming better. Stronger in mind. Stronger in body. Stronger in business. Stronger in relationships. Your life is not the culmination of your achievements. Your life is the achievement of your happiness.

Find joy in the journey. Stop trying to get to some end-destination. Enough money. A big enough house. A nice enough car. A long enough vacation. Those who dream and lust about these superficial things rarely achieve them. Whereas, those focus on the next step, serving their tribe, sharing their message, solving problems, continually designing their Character journey to transform themselves to become better. These end-destinations become a choice, a luxury, if they choose. (I drive a 2006 Nissan Xterra that has almost 200K miles on it. Could I buy a new Tesla? Sure. Would it make me any happier? Not one bit.)

The Tribe you build will be a reflection of the Values, Beliefs, and Convictions that you share. If you focus on superficial shit, you will attract others who *desire* that same superficial shit.

Trust me.

You don't want a tribe that focuses on superficial shit. Those are the simpletons. The opportunists. The get-rich-quick seekers.

Hard work.

Discipline.

The 1% Journey.

These are the *kinds of people* that are the most valuable to you; As friends. As readers. As future partners. Because they are the ones *committed* to putting in the work to transform their life.

Step 3 – Paid For Inspiring

I spent a lot of years allowing my Business to become my life, and frankly, it nearly destroyed my family. A much better approach I have found, is to turn my Life into my business.

Again, those two sentences:

1) ```
The game of money is a simple one. X's & O's. Add value, add wealth. That's the simple shit.
```

2) ```
The game of LIFE. That is the true genius. That is the real game to figure out and play.
```

The cool part is, with what we have discussed, by deliberately designing *the path* that your Character will travel, to transform himself. Then publishing that journey. You achieve #1 *by* mastering #2.

Every single person on earth is trying to figure out how to *play* this Game of LIFE.

But they're *stuck* in the 9-5 grind.

They're *stuck* in comparing themselves to others.

They're stuck in the belief that success *should* happen faster *and* be easier.

They're *stuck*…

They're *stuck*…

They're *stuck*…

So, what do you imagine is the greatest value that you could possibly deliver, to those people? Remember, the game of money is a simple one. X's & O's. Add value, add wealth. Not complicated…

In a world that is continually distracted, where people work, but never focus…

In a world that is connected but feels utterly alone.

In a world that is *depressed* due to an overwhelming amount of information and misdirection on a daily basis…

What is the greatest value we can deliver?

Add value, add wealth:

Belief...
Faith. And Clarity.

There is no greater value that we can deliver to a person than these things. 1) *Belief* that it is possible. 2) *Faith* to take that first step. And 3) a clear *Path* of exactly how to achieve as we have.

How did you become a full-time real estate investor?

How did you get in the best shape of your life?

How did you inspire your spouse and kids to make fitness a priority?

How did you build a such a lucrative online business?

How did you build a local movement that donated hundreds of thousands to local charities in your community?

How did you become a such a compelling *Storyteller*?

This, my friend, is where it all starts:

Delivering Value (AT SCALE)...

Story + Athlete = *Story*Athlete

Story = The Sport

Athlete = Elite Performance

Add value, add wealth:

A) How can you deliver *Belief* that what you achieved is *possible* for someone else, if you don't tell your stories?

B) How can you deliver *Faith,* that inspires people to *take* that critical first step, if you don't tell your stories?

C) How can you deliver a "clear *Path*" to achieve the *same* Transformative Result you achieved, if you don't tell your stories?

Turning your LIFE into your business is simple: 1) Live a Challenge-Based Life. Do hard shit. Stick with it. Get the transformative result. And 2, as a StoryAthlete, document the Journey...

1 – Do Hard Shit

2 – Stick With It

3 – Get The Result

People will ask, "What's your secret?"

= You will say, "Here's how I did it - *Go here...*"

= *Get Paid to Become Your Best Self*

STORYTELLER
Your LIFE is YOUR BUSINESS
Your AUDIENCE is THE MONETIZATION

Monetize your LIFE.

This is what StoryAthlete is about.

Your LIFE and BUSINESS are *not* separate: (Work-life balance = A failed concept)

Your LIFE *is* your business: (Work-life integration = Extreme leverage)

Again, everything I present in this book, I want to keep super simple because these concepts are not complex to execute. Simplicity is what StoryAthlete does best. Define the path, travel the path…

<u>I'm going to keep repeating this:</u>

Step 1 – Do Hard Shit

Step 2 – Stick With It

Step 3 – Get The Result

People will ask, "What's your secret?"

= You will say, "Here's how I did it - *Go here…*"

= *Get Paid to Become Your Best Self*

Endgame: Build The Audience

As you turn your LIFE into your business, it's not essential to own the product(s) or service(s) that you recommend.

It is far more critical that you *own* the relationship with the audience!

<u>The Reader-*Writer* Relationship</u>.

Here are the four (4) pillars of logic:

```
Logic #1 - True or False? (TRUE!)
```

PAY ATTENTION TO THE BUSINESS LEADERS YOU ADMIRE - They all have an audience, built by publishing stories. Their audience is what gives them power. Now look at the Business Owners, Service-providers, and Entrepreneurs who struggle daily, and live a life of quiet desperation? They have no audience. Because they failed to create properly structured content. StoryAthlete (+ Spiderweb Philosophy) - fixes that problem. Building folks into *true* Inspiring Characters.

```
Logic #2 - True or False? (TRUE!)
```

You find me a strong business, and I'll show you a connected audience that traveled this 6-step path: **1)** Sitcom-based content - binge watching, listening, reading. **2)** Binge consumption = Knowing the Character. **3)** Knowing the Character = The ability to

55

judge the Character. **4)** Control OPN (Own Personal Narrative) = Positive judgment of Character. **5)** Positive judgment = People know, like and trust the Character. **6)** The Character = YOU, who benefits from the 1,000 True Fan Philosophy.

Logic #3 - True or False? (TRUE!)

> **Write this down**: Audience + Offer = Money. If you want maximum profit; there are three (3) ingredients: Audience + Offer + Ongoing Communication. The strength of your "Offer" will affect your conversion. Either increase it or decrease it. The other two ingredients are 100% tied to your ability to create Sitcom-based content. If you create more Offers, your True Fans will be eager to invest in those, too!

Logic #4 - True or False? (TRUE!)

> *The Path* to 6 or 7-Figures Begins With 1,000 True Fans! Your job is not to sell your product or service. That is extremely shortsighted and the pursuit of the (lowly) salesperson. Thus, your job is to sell your values, beliefs, convictions. Your personal and business "religion," constructed into a set of Principles, so that *outsiders*, when they learn about you, convert to becoming a True Fan.

Should you be sufficiently interested, in becoming a StoryAthlete Partner, I will walk through the ENTIRE BUSINESS MODEL that we will GIVE to you, the complete PRODUCT-LINE, plus the SOFTWARE and COMMUNITY that makes getting the Transformative Result, from doing hard shit, automatic and certain:

1) Become a full-time real estate investor

Remember, our job is to do the hard shit, to get the *transformative* result, that creates *demand* for our designed path. Becoming a full-time real estate investor, for millions of people, is the ultimate dream job. This means, when you achieve it, if you haven't already, by following the path we *designed*,

people are going to ask you. "How did you do it?" **What is your secret?"** As a StoryAthlete Partner, you'll say, "Here's how – go here..." That partner link will create income for you that you *own* and recurring revenue. But let's talk about the *path*. Despite the bullshit that gets peddled by the charlatans and hucksters in the REI space. There are only four pieces to this puzzle. **1) Deal Flow. 2) Lead Conversion. 3) Funding & Structuring, and 4) Execution Team**. Compared to other businesses, the investing business is one of the simplest on earth. Which is good. Especially when you consider these advantages: A) The upside profit-potential is huge. Each deal we execute delivers a typical profit between $10K to $140K, depending on the asset and exit strategy. B) There are 12 ways to get paid as an *Asset Control Specialist*, so you're never pigeon-holed into forcing, like most investors, square pegs into round holes. That is how most investors *lose* really quickly. Not us!
C) Freedom of time. There is no client-work. There is no service work. As a full-time investor, you make the rules. You set your hours. You decide on the projects. Meaning, you can escape the client-trap and associated headaches. Plus, no longer are you trading time for money, "hour work, dollar earned," so you're free to live the kind of life that most folks *say* is impossible.

> **Don't start from scratch.** At every step, we provide guaranteed implementation of the business model. Use what we have built and provided. It works. It's proven. After the Asset Control Specialist class, next comes the Game of "List It or Flip It?" This concept took Bob Grand, our first beta-tester, from zero to over $500K in cash + equity in the first 12-months. Ron Nedd, a newbie to investing, followed instructions and did his first deal in 45 days, netting him $36K from a lead cost of $325 invested.

> > **This is not a coaching program.** This is a Partnership. For the typical coaching program, you will pay $10K to as much as $39K for a one-year program. And you won't get half the support that we provide in our Partner model. Nor will you get the 'Turn your *LIFE* into your business' blueprint, with complete product-line and support to execute it. Instead, you will be right back at square one. Chasing income. Rather than designing a life that creates leverage.

```
Add Value; Add Wealth: This is what most entrepreneurs don't understand.
Their focus is too narrow and shortsighted. Add-value, in the scope of real
estate investing, is simple to understand. We get paid to solve the problem
of the Frustrated Seller. That is one income stream. But. And this is
important. Lumber mills don't just get paid for their lumber, they get paid
for their saw dust, too. (This realization = free money)

     Our mission isn't to just get paid from the investing deal. We get paid
     to deliver Belief, Faith, and Clarity, too, to our audience of readers
     following our journey. To do this, we don't only control assets. We
     create assets, too. Case studies are Marketable assets. Advertising is
     how we build our audience, and thus, a lucrative online business.
```

2) Build a lucrative online business

Remember, our job is to do the hard shit, to get the *transformative* result, that creates *demand* for our designed path. Building a lucrative online business, for millions of people, is the ultimate dream job. This means, when you achieve it, by following the path we've *designed,* people are going to ask you. "How did you do it?" **What is your secret?"** As a StoryAthlete Partner, you'll say, "Here's how – *go here…*" That partner link will create income for you that you *own* and recurring revenue. But let's talk about the *path*. To build a lucrative online business, in most cases, you'd have to understand product-development. Direct-response copywriting. Offer structure. Then, to make your advertising work, you'd have to create well-converting upsells and down-sells. You'd have to write great copy. Build the funnel. Set up the payment gateways. Create the legal compliance. Have customer support. Setup and manage fulfillment services. Possibly hire. Manage employees. Set up Ops and automations. Etc. This list of *unseen tasks* and needed *skills* is why most never succeed in creating an online business that spits off streams of recurring revenue.

> **Our Partners don't have to do any of *this*!** We *all* have our skills and abilities. My skill and ability is online marketing. Direct-response copywriting. Building funnels that convert. Delivering information-products that people love. As a StoryAthlete Partner, these products, funnels, and assets, become yours. *Ready to use…*

> **YES, I WILL WALK YOU THROUGH EVERYTHING** – at least, those who are sufficiently interested in this opportunity to become a StoryAthlete Partner. I will show your inner-workings of our front- and back-end marketing system. Of our product-development process. *Everything*. The three phases of business; Acquisition, Ascension, Retention. The five phases of high-value asset creation: Message, offer, copy, funnels and traffic, Ops and automations.

> *Everything* **that we do. Becomes** *yours*. For every piece of the "Turn your *LIFE* into your business" blueprint, you will be provided the templates. You focus on 1) doing hard shit, 2) Sticking with it, 3) Getting the transformative result. And 4) Documenting your journey to create the Reader-*writer* relationship with your audience. To create True Fans. And we'll give you the product-line to monetize the shit out of *all* your hard work.

Later in this book, I will touch on the EXTREME LEVERAGE that an Open Source Community, truly delivers.

3) Get in the best physical shape of your life, while inspiring your spouse and kids to make fitness a priority in their life:

Remember, our job is to do the hard shit, to get the *transformative* result, that creates *demand* for our designed path. Looking good in the mirror, feeling confident and strong, thanks to a strong body, for millions of people, is a dream achievement. This means, when you achieve it, by following the path we have *designed*, people are going to ask. "How did you do it?" **What is your secret?"** As a StoryAthlete Partner, you'll say, "Here's how – *go here…*" That partner link will create income for you that you *own* and recurring revenue. But let's talk about the *path*. What good is the perfect-life; having time-freedom, financial security, thanks to recurring revenue, if we don't have our health, and the health of our family members? Mind. Body. Business. Relationships. "Fat Ryan" was 40-pounds overweight. He was a shitty human because he was tired, exhausted, and lethargic all the time. His kids would ask him, "Dad, do you want to play x, y, or z sport or *do* x, y, z physical activity? He said, "no, no, no." He was a shitty husband, too, because he had zero energy and a perpetually tired brain. He was an irritable dick. His wife got the *leftovers*, after a long day focused on business. And *what* was leftover, was fucking moldy. *But.* Reintroducing fitness as a *pillar* in my life (GRIT + FUEL) transformed everything. I lost 40-pounds. My energy levels went through the roof. My brain performance, and mental clarity, increased my output and productivity by at least 400%. Instead of completing 1 or 2-hours of Deep Work, I started completing 6-8 hours.

> **Entering *Flow State* was effortless**. The Lesser Self is sabotaged by a drained battery, i.e. brain, causing weak-brain decisions. The opposite of that is the Heroic Self. He trains his Mind, through the Body, as the elite *athlete* does for performance. The inability to focus goes away. Clarity takes over. And, instead of creating one asset a week or month, that can be leveraged to multiply ROT: Return on Time, the Heroic Self creates a *minimum* of one leverageable asset per day. Leveraged assets are what create time-freedom.

>> **A better husband**. I stopped working 10 to 12-hour days. I no longer needed to. By 4Xing productivity, through *Peak Energy* and mental focus, I could work a fraction of the hours and still achieve more. This created time to focus on my wife. To be thoughtful. To be caring. At the same time, the business grew stronger, too. (btw, the sex is better, also! ;-)

>> **A better father**. There are so many *life lessons* that a parent can teach their kids through fitness.

Through Family Fitness: "Those who suffer together, Bond Together."

4) Impact your community, by creating a movement, to donate hundreds-of-thousands to local charities:

Remember, our job is to do the hard shit, to get the *transformative* result, that creates *demand* for our designed path. <u>Being the leader of a local movement, that donates tens of thousands each quarter, to local charities, for millions of people, is a *position* of envy. This means, when you achieve it, by following the path we have *designed*, people are going to ask you. "How did you do it?" **What is your secret?"** As a StoryAthlete Partner, you'll say, "Here's how – *go here…*" That partner link will create income for you that you *own* and recurring revenue. But let's talk about the *path*. Through becoming an ImpactClub® (IC) cofounder, you have the ability to achieve this in your community. The first *IC* launched on December 19th, 2016, in Northern Virginia. 112 members attend that first event. In January of 2017, the next *IC* launched. This time, from our 28-day launch campaign, 181 new members attend that first event. Donating over $18K to the winning local charity. The next month, in February 2017, we launched the third IC with Eric Verdi. At that event, 182 new members attended. Again, donating over $18K to the winning charity. This continued. <u>Since then, we have dialed in every aspect of launching, running, and managing a local ImpactClub® as the leader of a local movement.</u>

From No one to Someone, *almost* overnight! – <u>Almost every cofounder we have launched with, has earned their community's award for distinguished citizen or philanthropist</u>. To date, Bob Grand, our IC® Eugene cofounder, leads a movement that has donated more than $125K to local charities. Eric Verdi, our IC® Frederick cofounder, leads a local movement (over 300 members) that has donated over $380K to local charities. Mike Turner, our IC® Boise cofounder, leads a movement that has donated more than $275K to local charities. Each are *known as* a "Community Leader" and "Philanthropist." <u>If you're intelligent and understand *positioning*, and how it creates trust, I don't have to tell you the *value* of those Reputations.</u> When operating in a Negative Reputation industry, they immediately differentiate you from the *negative* stereotype. Bob Grand, as a *Philanthropist*, gets many investment deals that other investors don't get, because he has *superior* positioning. Thus, *superior* trust.

<u>There is a 12-month "Demonstrate your Character" period before you can *apply* to launch an ImpactClub®</u> - For the true Partner and person of Character, this shouldn't be a problem at all. This requirement not only protects the reputation of ImpactClub® and our cofounders. But, when you become a cofounder, protects you, too.

<u>We've spent hundreds-of-thousands to dial in every aspect of this LEGACY model.</u>

5) Everything above is MADE POSSIBLE by your *ability* to craft sitcom-based content, as a Storyteller, to *own* the relationship with your audience, to enjoy the financial security (a high 6- or 7-figue income), thanks to just 1,000 true fans.

Remember, our job is to do the hard shit, to get the *transformative* result, that creates *demand* for our designed path. Being an inspiring storyteller, who can weave words into influential and persuasive arguments, for millions of people, is a skill they envy. This means, when you achieve it, by following the path we have *designed*, people are going to ask you. "How did you do it?" **What is your secret?**" As a StoryAthlete Partner, you'll say, "Here's how – *go here…*" That partner link will create income for you that you *own* and recurring revenue. But let's talk about the *path*. If you have consumed the first 10 episodes of the *StoryAthlete* Podcast, then you know that storytelling is everything. It's the communication *tool* of leaders. It's the *leverage* to create intellectual property assets. It's the *catalyst* that speeds up the creation of trust. It's the *skill* that creates movements. It's the *teacher* that conveys the most powerful lessons. Great storytelling is the *foundation* of great marketing. Great books. Great videos. Great podcasts. Great email newsletters. Great social media feeds. Great offers and sales pitches. Stories are the true currency of our society, because *Stories* are what secure and keep people's attention. My friend, *owning the attention*, listen to the podcast, is how we achieve financial security. He who *owns* the attention of the market, wins. Marketing, i.e. new client acquisition, is all about *owning* the attention. Ascension and retention, too, is at least 80-90% about keeping that *owned* attention. When you lose *that* attention, you lose the interest, support, and loyalty, of your customers, clients, users, or members.

> **Review the (4) Pillars of Logic.** You can review those four pillars by flipping back a few pages. Accepting them is what *unlocks* the opportunities that most never experience. There is nothing more powerful to an entrepreneur, than YOU, the storyteller, who owns their own audience. Financially, it's damn hard to fuck up, when 1) you have people who love you, and 2) who are eager to buy whatever offer you create next. *True Fans*!

> > **It starts with GRIT.** A proven path. Storytelling is not easy. But we have developed a training regimen that makes it easy. Heroic Self vs. Lesser Self. Quite literally, we write the Character we want to become *into* existence. Then comes the Game of IODs, to create and control OPN: own personal narrative. Then comes *Spiderweb Philosophy*.

Spiderweb Philosophy is how we create ENTIRE business(es), and MULTIPLE product-line(s), purely around your Message!

As I wrote early in this book, back on page 5, it takes a friend to call you on your shit. But I'm not here to call you on your shit, because a good Partner and teammate, knows when they need to call themselves on their shit.

Neither Sloper, nor I are here to sell you (or anyone else).

StoryAthlete is a *Path* to turn your *LIFE* into your business. To get paid to become your best self.

StoryAthlete is a *Partnership*.

StoryAthlete is a community ruled by *Open Source*.

As a Partner, we each accept responsibility to do our part, to make sure we rapidly advance innovation.

TRUTH #3
Proven Frameworks (Combat Failure & Disease)

Your partnership in StoryAthlete, should you apply, and be accepted. I assure you, won't be like any other experience you've ever had. Not only do we *think* different. We *behave* different...

MOST PEOPLE <u>FAIL</u> FOR THREE REASONS:

Either 1) They're too scared to *do* hard shit. (success isn't a "pretty" sport)

2) They *don't* stick with it. (they quit early, and often)

Or 3) They implemented and executed a *flawed* model from the start.

Before we address these reasons, we should get clear on *why* it matters to you <u>that</u> - they get addressed...

Are you *legacy* motivated? Do you want your life to matter? Does self-actualization, reaching your highest potential mean anything to you?

Being vs. Becoming => YOU vs.(Future) YOU: Two quotes have stuck with me over the years, and both have to do with becoming. The first is: "I've always believed that the definition of hell is reaching the end of your life and coming face-to-face with the person that you *might* have been." Yep, that would be my hell. All that potential, and I never tapped it. What a shame that would be. What kind of example would *that* set for my kids? And the second, from Churchill, "To each, there comes *in their lifetime* a special moment when they are figuratively tapped on the shoulder and offered the chance to do a very special thing, unique to them and fitted to their talents. What a tragedy *if* that moment finds them unprepared or unqualified for that *which could have been* their finest hour." I believe my journey right now, to "Become…" hard(er) to kill; mentally, physically, financially is the preparation for that *particular moment* that lies ahead. I would hate for what could have been my finest hour, to be the *hour* of my greatest regret.

ON JUDGEMENT DAY (Being vs. Becoming). On the day I die, at my funeral, I hope the question gets asked, "Did Ryan Fletcher have the courage to fight to achieve his highest potential to the very end? Or, was he too much of a fucking coward to pursue it?" Then, one by one, I hope people stand to give their testimony. "He fought for it." "He fought for it." "He fought for it." I don't want people to say this because it's my funeral. Or because they feel *some need* to pay any unwarranted respect or sympathy. I don't need anyone's fucking sympathy. If people say it, I want it to be because - that *truth*: "He fought for it." Was self-evident. This too, will serve as the demonstration to my kids, "Your Dad never gave up on, never settled, and never was he *too afraid* to chase down his highest potential."

LEGACY ASSET (Preservation of Memories). When most of society thinks about legacy, and what it is, most people think in terms of monetary assets. Or in terms of public recognition. A library or something built in their name or honor. Me, I think in terms of *memories* preserved. My life, and therefore my *legacy*, is a collection of my experiences. Monetary assets will get spent, sold, or exchanged. Money comes and goes. So, who cares? You can lose it, make more of it. Money isn't invaluable. So, more valuable than the money I have, will be the *memories* and lessons *preserved* in my stories. Today, I am 38-years old. From my childhood, I have but only a handful of memories. Occasionally, something pops up that I remember. But mostly, when I think back to the days of "Little Ryan," nothing specific comes to mind. The struggle of my parents' first 40 years has been lost because a) I don't remember much of those specifics, and b) they didn't preserve those memories *through* writing their stories. My parents are nearly 70-years old. I would love nothing more than to be able to open a book, written by my 38-year-old Mom, or Dad (from 30+ years ago), to be able to *SEE* the world from their eyes, as they experienced it. As my kids will be able to see the world *as* I saw it. But that is a *Legacy Asset* they never created. So, I can't. My kids, I'm making sure of it, will not be deprived of that ability. When they decide to read my stories,

> they will be there waiting. From beyond the grave, I will be there to encourage and inspire. To uplift and push. To love and hug. To listen and give advice. Just from the IODs written, I have content for 4-plus books, and a new one planned every ninety to 120 days. Gary Vaynerchuk *films* his Character Journey, his *legacy*. I write mine.
>
> **LEGACY: (To ignite Lights).** I have long stated. My purpose in life is "to create a movement of movements, by helping others to create their own." A movement is nothing more than a connection to a message. Some movements grow to become large. Some remain small. Size does not define a movement. The depth of the shared conviction does. I am here to be a Light to those who find themselves in the Dark. And my Light is different from yours. And your Light is different from the hundreds of other Lights in the StoryAthlete community. Each is capable of reaching a different Dark place. Capable of creating a new ripple effect. Therefore, I exist to ignite, Lights. And I hope each newly lit Light (yours) goes on to become much brighter than my own.

As you can see: *WHY* it matters to me that those *causes*-of-failure get addressed, isn't trivial.

When I die, only my *documented* stories and the people *impacted* by my message, and through the d*emonstration* of my life, will remain. And like you, I only get one life, one shot to get it right…

To *not* live up to my potential:

That is…

My Greatest Fear!

Some people reading this *still* think StoryAthlete is about making more money. And, it is. But far more than that, StoryAthlete is about transforming our self to demonstrate to others *what* is possible…

If you have kids, you know they are ***watching*** your every move.

What you tell them to do - ***is not*** what they will do.

What *you* do - is ***what*** they will model.

Our kids witness *EVERYTING* – and they're constructing *models* (to emulate):

They witness how we think.

They witness how we behave.

They witness what we achieve.

They witness our habits (as well as our *limiting* beliefs).

They witness our mental toughness.

They witness whether or not we quit, and how often we quit.

Most parents think it is their *job* to tell their kids how to become successful, and happy, productive, contributing members of society. *That*, though, is false. Great parents *demonstrate* it.

In other words, don't listen to me.

Watch me.

This is how you build a business.

This is how you invest in real estate.

This is how you achieve peak energy and peak physical fitness.

This is how you optimize for mental performance.

This is how you lead a movement that donates hundreds-of-thousands to charities.

This is how you craft your message.

This is how you tell your stories.

This is how you publish your stories into books.

This is how you turn your LIFE into your business.

This is how you get paid to become your best self. (1, 2, 3…)

This is how your purpose becomes your legacy.

This is how you serve the relationships *in your life* that matter most to you!

This is how you become…

Hard(er) to kill;
Mentally. Physically. Financially!

That is the job of StoryAthlete. That is the mission. The purpose. The calling. To make every member of our Community, hard(er) to kill; mentally, physically, financially, to best *serve* our loved ones.

Our *selfish* desire to optimize our personal performance; Mind, Body, and Business, is what enables us to be "the Rock" to the Relationships in our life, to *selflessly* serve those we love most…

Our kids.

Our spouse.

Our communities.

If impacting these things doesn't mean shit to you, then why bother to *solve* these (3) causes of failure:

Either 1) They're too scared to *do* hard shit. (success isn't a "pretty" sport)

2) They *don't* stick with it. (they quit early, and often)

Or 3) They implemented and executed a *flawed* model from the start.

Solving these means EVERYTHING to me! (I'll explain why)

Add value; Add wealth;

How do we add value?

Deliver *Belief*, *Faith*, and *Clarity*.

How do we arrive at Clarity?

Through research and a scientific process:

Step 1 – Identify The Problem

Let's reverse engineer it.

As a pre-med student, even though I failed to get into medical school, and got rejected 47 times over a 4-year period, I did learn: Before there can be a prescription, there must be a diagnosis.

And, to arrive at a diagnosis, we must look at the symptoms:

Everything, for the most part, is cause and effect.

If you can figure out the symptoms, and understand the cycle, then you can start to understand the underlying cause(s):

Problem #1 – They're too scared to *do* hard shit.

Good news: Not much we can do for this person. This person doesn't belong inside of StoryAthlete. The desire and choice to do hard shit, requires one of two things to be true: 1) Some people are just *wired* to want to take on the biggest challenges. The harder the better. The scarier the better. They're *wired* that way. Maybe they're adrenaline junkies. Or masochists. I don't know. And some aren't. <u>If a person isn't, then to sufficiently motivate them, to choose to do hard shit, number 2) must be present. Which is: The PAIN of staying in the same place, remaining stagnant, must be greater than the FEAR they have about moving forward</u>. If that tremendous pain and dissatisfaction isn't present, then that person will *never* move from their comfort zone. And, it's a lost cause to try to convince them to do hard shit, when 1) they aren't wired that way. Or 2) Aren't sufficiently motivated to escape the Pain/Dissatisfaction of their current place in life.

COMPLACENCY DESTROYS LEGACY. In the book, "How The mighty Fail," by Jim Collins. He speaks about how "Good is the enemy of great." Which is true. Don't wait for perfection. Get started. Create that MVP (minimum viable product). Bring the idea to market. The problem is: Good, when it's not great, becomes commoditized. Innovation doesn't happen. Soon, good isn't sufficient. <u>Complacency, staying in the comfort zone, ends up destroying the entity. Complacency doesn't just destroy a business, either. Complacency destroys the Mind. The mindset. The person. The body. Our relationships. Greatness requires sustained, deliberate intensity</u>. In other words, do hard shit and *keep* doing it often. By constantly pushing up against our limits is how we grow, is how we innovate! It's how our *legacy* gets cemented! <u>The opposite of growth, created by choice, is the Lesser Self</u>. That's the *side of us* that sabotages.

Sometimes a person who is *too scared* to do hard shit, can be inspired by others who are perpetually pushing up against their limits. The growth in *them* is WHAT inspires that person to replicate *their* behaviors.

Problem #2 - They *don't* stick with it.

This one is more intriguing because, at this point, they chose to do hard shit. They got started. But then, time and time again, they stopped. Gave up. And quit.

THE CYCLE OF MISERY. Have you ever heard of this? Have you experienced it? Pay close attention. This is the painful path that many entrepreneurs travel. They start off with a spirit of optimism. They have high hopes. They are excited to be starting something new. The vision is there. The possibilities are endless. It could be starting a real estate investment business or any other kind of venture. The first month, or two months, is great. Progress is happening. You're in the build-phase. You're planning the next steps. You're designing how everything is going to work. It all seems to work flawlessly. You can practically see yourself being rich, and happy, and retiring on a beach somewhere. THEN IT HAPPENS. Progress stops. The excitement is gone. Everything got hard all of a sudden. Despite all the planning, and goalsetting, execution never happens. Implementation never happens. Every day, every step, it feels like your slogging through quicksand. Every task ends up taking 6X as long it should. And costs, it seems, 10X more than expected. It wasn't supposed to be this way. Frustration sets in. Two months have passed. Five months have passed. A year or two passes. And because you feel like you should be further along by now. You start to stress. You try to catch up. You try to work faster. This turns that frustration about not being further along into Overwhelm. The more overwhelmed you get the more frustrated you get. The more Frustrated and Overwhelmed you get, the more Depressed you get. That depression builds up. Fuck it! Why even try! I'm a pathetic failure. Other people can do it, why can't I? It's not hard for them. Why am I so stupid? FODQ: Frustration. Overwhelm. Depression, and Quit. That is the cycle of misery. It is painfully predictable.

> **THE "TRIO" OF NEGATIVE CYCLES.** In the next section, (addressing Problem #3) "They implemented and executed a *flawed* model from the start," we'll take a detailed look at the three negative cycles that feed the "Cycle of Misery." Here and now, though, let's address the other two connected factors:
>
>> **GREENER PASTURES.** This is why I hate, and have great disdain for, The Guru Party. These are the trainers and coaches who perpetually sell folks on the new, better, different, far superior way of doing something. Every day, it's a new shiny object. No emphasis put on the foundations. They don't reinforce the basics. If I want to ensure *that people fail*, this is all I'd need to do. Continually *distract* them. Continually *put* new and different temptations

> in front of them. After all: Why implement something that is hard, difficult, or challenging, when I can buy something that is *promised to be* easier, better, faster, and more effective? This behavior, motivated by the temptations put in front of them by the Guru Party, is what keeps people traveling the Cycle of Misery, year after year. This lack of effective progress makes them desperate.
>
> **DESPERATION**. A desperate entrepreneur is a self-destructive entrepreneur. Because a desperate person is solely focused on survival. They're out of money. They're out of time. They need fast, easy, quick results. So, instead of behaving as an intelligent entrepreneur, they behave as a get-rich-quick seeker. Chasing instant gratification. They reach and grab for whatever life-raft is closest. Often climbing over and drowning their loved ones in the process.

If you accept these 15 Words, EVERYTHING you want can be yours: "Everything you want in life can be had, *IF*... You just stop quitting on yourself." Embrace that, and you earn a one-way ticket off "The Cycle of Misery." Instead of FODQ, you FINISH and achieve!

- Achieve: Living *life* on your terms as a full-time real estate investor.
- Achieve: Being in the *best* physical shape of your life.
- Achieve: Thankful, for having *inspired* your family to prioritize health and fitness
- Achieve: Financial security, having built an *ultra*-profitable online business.
- Achieve: The power of a *connected* audience, having built 1000 true fans!
- Achieve: Donating tens-of-thousands to local charities each quarter.
- Achieve: Turned your *LIFE* into your business!!
- Etc…

All of this happens automatically, *unless*:

Problem #3 - They implemented and executed a *flawed* model from the start.

> **Do hard shit. Stick with it. Get the result.** If *that* is all that is required, to become self-actualized, to live the life that we envisioned, then why is it that so many never achieve it? Exactly, right. They choose to do hard shit, but then don't stick with it (Problem #2). So, they end up traveling the Cycle of Misery. Staying on that train, year after year. *FODQ*. Until,

they finally submit, give up, and settle. To quote Thoreau, "Most men live a life of quiet desperation." Or, to borrow from Franklin. "Some people die at 25 but aren't buried until 75." The sentiment is the same. A person can only take so much punishment, misery, failure. Before they *finally* just accept mediocrity as the best they can do. To see people, give up on themselves in this fashion, is heartbreaking. So, how do we get people off the Cycle of Misery? It starts by understanding the three negative cycles that feed the cycle of Misery.

FLAWED MODELS: To arrive at a non-flawed model, you have to ask, and then solve, a bunch of questions: Do I have the proper design? Have I secured the proper talent? Do I have the needed skills? Do I have the required resources? Have I mapped out the blueprint? Have I engineered the design? Have I prioritized the proper steps of execution? Have I determined my content strategy? Have I crystalized my message? Have I determined my distribution strategy? Have I built my marketing systems? What if nothing goes as planned, do I have a contingency in place? What if that contingency plan doesn't work, have I designed a method of continual iteration? Do I have relationships or partnerships with experts, who I can turn to? If I end up needing an immediate answer, how will I get it? Most entrepreneurs, I can tell you, don't design their model of execution, hardly at all, so they end up forced to navigate in the dark, under the low light of a half-moon, without a compass. Being unprepared in this *Darkness*, fuels the Cycle of Misery.

Part 1) The Cycle of Staying Small. Remember FODQ: Frustration. Overwhelm. Depression. Quit. To get off the Cycle of Misery, we must prevent this chain of events from happening. What causes frustration? Lack of progress. There is too much work. And not enough time. The solution to this is to design *leverage* into the system. If you had 12 employees, instead of just you, now could you get all that work completed to see faster progress? Of course. Except, maybe you can't afford the overhead of hiring 12 employees. So, what's the alternative? Assets. Ops & automations. Software and systems. Most entrepreneurs stay small, hoping to build a big business one day, with a high-income, but never do because their days are spent doing activities. Activities though, are not Assets. Assets can get leveraged. Build it once. They work forever. Or at least, for years.

Take this book, for example, that you are reading right now. As I type this paragraph, I've worked on it for 9 days. About 6 hours per day. That's 54-hours so far. I have approx 4 days left before I complete this book. So, in total, at that rate, I'll have 78-hours invested. Once complete, though, I don't ever have to write it again. It's done. It's an intellectual property asset. It's an oil well. Turn it on. Watch it work. This one book can do the work of a hundred salespeople. It works around the clock 24/7. It doesn't take days off. It never calls in sick. It never has a bad day. Once someone requests information about the StoryAthlete Partner program, out this book goes. And through other built Assets;

sales funnels, fulfillment processes, software integrations, etc., it's all automated and requires none of my time.

ROT (Return on time) LEADS TO ROI: Most entrepreneurs are so focused on creating a strong ROI: return on investment, they never think about how to architect a strong ROT: return on time. And because they run out of time, they can only work so many hours in a day, they get frustrated by the fact, they can never get *done* all the work that needs to get done. So, progress STALLS. They hit a ceiling. They're working so many hours at this point, because of all that work, that needs to get done, their BUSINESS has become their LIFE. They're stressed. They're tired. They're exhausted. Their relationships get strained. Frustration leads to Overwhelm. Overwhelm leads to depression. Depression leads to quitting. Settling. Succumbing. And a life of hard work and mediocrity is the result. ROI never happens, because ROT never happened.

Prioritize Assets. Asset creation is how you maximize ROT: return on time, which maximizes ROI. Which gives you the time-freedom and capital to get yourself off the Cycle of Staying Small. (As a StoryAthlete Partner, inside our ecosystem, you'll be instructed of how to do this. But also, be surrounded by others who prioritize it).

Part 2) The Cycle of Missed Opportunities. The COST of missed opportunities in business is massive. Especially in the industries of; Real Estate Investing and Online Business. The opportunities that don't get capitalized on, that could get capitalized on, costs entrepreneurs millions. Literally, millions in opportunity cost. There are TWO reasons for why this happens: 1) The person lacks necessary expertise, resulting in a lack of confidence to pull the trigger to move forward. Or 2) That person lacks the necessary resources and or connections to execute on *what* he knows is a homerun. Think about real estate investing, for example. You find this great property. It represents a massive opportunity. But then, something puts you outside of your wheelhouse in terms of knowledge and comfort. This creates a delay. This creates a hesitation. Should I, or shouldn't I? Before you know it, the opportunity is missed. The opportunity is lost. Potentially, tens-of-thousands down the drain. Or in building an online business, you have a great idea that you *KNOW* will help people. But, when it comes time to execute, you're not sure how to convert that idea into a saleable product. Nor are you sure how to write the copy or build the sales funnel to sell that product. Again, the opportunity is missed. It dies. Potentially, hundreds-of-thousands down the drain. Because that great idea you had, never gets executed.

FEAR. UNCERTAINTY. SELF-DOUBT. These are the forces that drive The Cycle of Missed Opportunities. Sure, sometimes "luck" and "timing" play into the equation, too. 'Wrong place, wrong time.' But those are rare incidents. Not the most common causes of missed opportunities. Fear. Uncertainty. Self-doubt. These are the things that lead to delay, procrastination, paralysis-by-analysis. And most often, and most costly, just the lack of implementation and execution of that steps and tasks that you know need to be executed.

TIME OR PARTNER: To solve those drivers above, this is the choice. Pay in time. Or Partner with people or networks of people, who have strengths in the area of your weaknesses. It's just a fact: Skill and experience, to create expertise and confidence, takes time. It takes years. Author Malcolm Gladwell wrote the book *Outliers*, where he talks about the 10,000-hour rule. Practice is the path to mastery. 10,000-hours equals 20-hours per week for ten years. The problem is, until that practice builds into skill, and that skill builds into mastery – year after year – a massive amount of frustration begins to fester from one missed opportunity after another. This creates the cascade of FODQ. The alternative to ten years of practice, to achieve mastery, is to partner with those who have the skill and expertise and or the resources and connections in the specific areas you are weak.

EGO & GREED: For lots of people partnering isn't an option, though, because they're greedy. They refuse to share in the upside. They want it all for themselves. Or their ego demands all the credit for the outcome or achievement. To build any kind of online business, for example. I give our Partners complete access, and every detail of our CAF: Class Acquisition Funnel blueprint. Every step has been proven out. I even give our Partners the product-line to go with it. For some, though, they refuse to use it because they want the credit of "knowing they forged" their own way. I call that stupidity. But hey – to each their own. Same applies on the real estate investing side. Sloper is a masterful partner to partner with; deal flow, funding, deal structure, risk-mitigation protocols, risk management. But for some – they don't want to partner because they want to feel like they're self-made. Ego, greed, and people's pride, definitely *fuel* The Cycle of Missed Opportunities.

Venture Capital Firms. Most of the prominent venture capital firms, won't invest in a single founder company. Because single-founder companies tend to fail at a much higher rate. <u>There is simply too much work to get done. And not enough time or talent, when only a single founder is driving the company forward. The prominent venture capital firms most typically invest in 2-4 founder companies.</u> By Partnering, by combining different expertise, skills, talents, and abilities, the likelihood of success goes way up.

Part 3) The Cycle of Mistakes. Of the three (3) negative cycles that feed "The Cycle of Misery," this is the most devastating; toppling the FODQ dominos the fastest. This is the cycle that typically breaks the camel's back. Frustration, at this point, has been festering. <u>They have been stuck in "The Cycle of Staying Small." So, as a hailmary, they start to press. They get impatient. Start taking risks, and gambling, beyond their skill or ability. Fear. Uncertainty. Paralysis-by-analysis. They have been stuck in "The Cycle of Missed Opportunities," too. They have hit their breaking point. So, determined to move forward. They take a chance. They step up to the plate. They push their chips into the middle. They swing.</u> And fuck - they miss. Just like that. They lost their chips. They bet wrong. This is "The Cycle of Mistakes." And not only is it extremely costly, from a financial perspective. But the time-cost, too, of having to tear down and rebuild, or re-do, what was done, because it was wrong, is demoralizing. And disheartening.

> **FEAR OF LOSS (AGAIN):** Once someone swings *big* and misses, this does real damage in terms of their psychological mindset. They invested in their first fix-and-flip, for example, and botched it. Their numbers were wrong. Their estimates were off. Their scope of work incorrect. Their O-Zone not calculated. Their contractor screwed them. The renovation took 2X as long. Went 50% over budget. This doubled their holding costs. <u>One domino after another. Oh shit, oh shit, oh shit. Instead of making $30K net, they lost $10K-$20K or barely broke even, after 90 to 180 days of work.</u> We see it all the time. Rookies, beginners, approaching the game all wrong.
>
> > **LOST TIME (AGAIN, AND AGAIN):** In building an online business, this is the major penalty. People don't risk huge amounts of money. They risk huge amounts of time. In building their product. <u>In designing their sales funnels. In determining their KPIs. In crafting their message. In writing their copy. They do it wrong. They do it wrong. They do it wrong. One mistake after another. A year passes. Two years pass. Five years pass.</u> Frustration rages. They stop. Then they start again. Then they stop. They're perpetually overwhelmed at this point. Finally, the last two dominos fall…
> >
> > > **DEPRESSION & QUIT.** And now, they start over. *Again!* Or, they don't. They succumb. Mediocrity becomes their life. And *shackled* friend.

Problem #1 - They're too scared to *do* hard shit.
Problem #2 - They *don't* stick with it.
Problem #3 - They implemented and executed a *flawed* model from the start.

Consequence of Problem #1 – That person *Never* gets in the game!

Consequence of Problem #2 – FODQ: "The Cycle of Misery," over and over.

Consequence of Problem #3 – Everything works *against* you! – Feeding FODQ!

1) The Cycle of Staying Small
2) The Cycle of Missed Opportunities
3) The Cycle of Mistakes

The fact is, most people in life, in business, in health & fitness, in their relationships, are perpetual quitters. They don't see themselves, in most cases, as quitters. But *that* is what they have become.

<u>Was *becoming a quitter* their intention?</u>

NO.

But everything *is* Cause and Effect.

If you don't solve the problems that *feed* FODQ, then the last domino, "QUIT," becomes the only end possibility.

They stay broke.

Or they stay *working* more and more hours to make a better income.

Their *business* becomes their life.

They never *become* who they envisioned becoming.

Their relationships crumble around them.

- A mediocre spouse.

- A mediocre parent.

- A mediocre mind.

With *mediocre* health and fitness.

They work their *entire lives* to get somewhere new, somewhere better. But, never arrive at that end destination.

Step 2 – **Decide On Treatment**

<u>I told you, let's reverse engineer it.</u>

If success and happiness and fulfillment are *truly* cause and effect, and they are, then for every action there is a consequence.

And for every problem, there is a solution.

<u>Step 1</u> – Identify the Problem (we did that.)

<u>Step 2</u> – Decide on Treatment

Some people don't want treatment: For the first eighteen years of my life, my Dad was a smoker. He smoked a pack a day for 30 years. He smoked in the house, mainly in one room. At night, when you looked in that room, after dinner, you could barely see to the other side. That's how thick the smoke was. My brother and I, when watching TV in that room with my Dad, laid on the floor. Smoke rises. We army crawled in and out of that room. <u>For as long as I can remember, my Mom, my brother, my sister, and myself, pleaded with my Dad to stop smoking. Our efforts did no good. Our requests fell on deaf ears. He didn't want treatment. Lots of alcoholics and addicts, despite the begging from loved ones, they don't want treatment</u>. Lots of people have lived in and known mediocrity *for so long* that they have developed a *fear* of success - yes! - this is a real thing. Success, in this case, is not their mission or goal. It is their nightmare. I don't know why this is. I can't explain it. And most of the people who self-sabotage as a means to *stay* in that place of mediocrity, familiarity, comfort-zone, etc., often do so *because* success terrifies them.

Greater responsibility: Maybe it's the greater responsibility and higher expectation that they fear that often comes with success. Again, I don't know. I just know, like my Dad. Like lots of alcoholics and addicts. They don't want treatment. Wrapped in a warm blanket of mediocrity and "This is how it's always been" is where they are most comfortable. And some people, *just* don't have our ambition. The masses vs. the 5%. <u>They don't care about legacy and purpose or mission. They just want to be able to BBQ on Saturdays. And catch the football game on Sundays</u>. If that makes them happy, great! - but those people don't want change. They want comfort, familiarity, and the predictable schedule of holding a standard nine-to-five. <u>To us, that is prison.</u>

I decided long ago...

ME?

...for the *disease* of mediocrity, and *cause* FODQ...

I wanted treatment.

Problem #1 - They're too scared to *do* hard shit.
Problem #2 - They *don't* stick with it.
Problem #3 - They implemented and executed a *flawed* model from the start.

Consequence of Problem #1 – That person *Never* gets in the game!

Consequence of Problem #2 – FODQ: "The Cycle of Misery," over and over.

Consequence of Problem #3 – Everything works *against* you! – Feeding FODQ!

1) The Cycle of Staying Small
2) The Cycle of Missed Opportunities
3) The Cycle of Mistakes

Once those problems are SOLVED!...

1 – Do Hard Shit

2 – Stick With It

3 – Get The Result

People will ask, **"What's your secret?"**

= You will say, "Here's how I did it - *Go here...*"

= *Get Paid to Become Your Best Self*

Some of you reading this, assume, I have written this book for you, as a sales letter to become a StoryAthlete Partner. Sorry, my friend, I have not. For my kids, I've written this book to sell them on a *Path*.

Whether you or the next person that reads this book becomes my Partner, makes zero difference to me.

I *don't* write for you.

I write for me. (it's my own form of therapy)

And I write for my kids.

At the end of my life, assuming a long life, I will have spent over 80-years trying to figure out how to play this game called life.

Again, those two sentences:

1) The game of money is a simple one. X's & O's. Add value, add wealth. That's the simple shit.

2) The game of LIFE. That is the true genius. That is the real game to figure out and play.

And, I don't want all of the lessons that I've learned in the past 30-years, and over the next 60-years, through my pain, and suffering, and misery. And through my happiness, focus, and purpose, to *die* when I die.

I recently read Matthew McConaughey's book, *Greenlights*.

It is the *stories* of his life.

I thought to myself, what an amazing *gift* to his kids.

My kids will have that *same* gift.

So, if you think I'm writing for you, to you, please understand that I am not. This is a book for my kids, as they become young adults.

I will publish many books of my writings, for them, and about them, too.

My LIFE is my business.

My LIFE exists - to be a *demonstration* to my kids!

Why does your LIFE exist?

Step 3 – The Prescription

What do you want?

Do you want the *Path* (and every detail) to become a full-time real estate investor?

Done!

Want the *Path* (and exact steps) to build an *ultra*-profitable online business?

Done!

77

Want the *Path* to get in the best physical shape of your life?

Done!

Want the *Path* to lead a local movement to donate tens-of-thousands to charities?

Done!

Want the *Path* to persuade, influence, and to be able to *inspire* with your words?

Done!

Want the *Path* to enjoy 1,000 True Fans?

Done!

<u>Want the *Path* to get PAID to become your best self?</u>

Done!

<u>But here's the real question</u>, what are you willing to sacrifice?

TRUTH #4
Sacrifice Is Required (= A Good Partner)

I'm so exhausted by the people who *want* things, but then aren't willing to *sacrifice* what is necessary to achieve them.

I can give you every *detail* to achieve the "wants" above.

Giving the "details" is the easy part.

Each day of each week, Sloper holds a LIVE CALL to review investment deals. And to answer any question that any Partner has, about real estate investing, from his experience, from our business.

Want…everything we have?

All of our systems and processes?

Done!

Each day, too, I do the same. Holding a LIVE CALL on the execution of the 5-phases to build high-value assets for your business. And to answer any question that any Partner has, about those phases.

Want…all of my templates *and* frameworks?

Want the entire *StoryAthlete* product-line as your own? (Income vs. Business)

Done!

<u>But</u> - what are you willing to sacrifice?

CRISPR:
(Editing "defective" genes)

In the opening if this letter, I wrote, "If you want to change your world, you have to change how you see it."

Specifically, I wrote this paragraph:

> From this point forward, we shall see your life as a string of DNA. To improve your DNA, we must knock out defective genes. And knock-in new superior genes. (<u>Keep reading, there are 7 "gene sequences" that cause people to never live up to their potential in life. Should we replace these "gene sequences," with new superior "gene sequences", our potential gets achieved.</u>)

In case you aren't familiar with CRISPR; this is a protein that is found in our cells, and possesses the ability, researchers have found. To cut our DNA, and can be programmed, to replace genes.

Also, known as "Genetic Engineering."

Is this legal?

Is this ethical?

Well, let's play a little game of *what if*?

> <u>If you were the parent of a child that had a genetic disease, that limited your child's life and potential</u>. And you knew, the CRISPR protein could be programmed by researchers, to knock-out a "defective gene" and knock-in new "proper gene," as the cure. To what *extent* would you go to get ***your child*** that treatment?
>
> *No* **gene editing** = a short, Miserable life.
>
> *With* gene editing = a New, amazing quality of life!

Personally, I would *go* to the end of the earth.

GENETIC ENGINEERING

In the context of everything we have discussed so far, there are (7) gene sequences that keep people from living up to their potential.

(7) gene sequences - that **keep** people *stunted*.

That **keep** people - *limited*.

Defective Gene		Superior Gene
I	vs.	D
NC	vs.	C
ND	vs.	D
SE	vs.	SD
NG	vs.	G
NP	vs.	P
AQ	vs	NQ

That's it.

Those (7) sequences are they only thing that separate the 'haves' from the 'have nots,' differentiating the people who:

1) Do hard shit,
2) Stick with it,
3) Get the *transformative* result…

Versus those who don't.

And, if you "edit" those (7) genes, swapping "defective" for "superior," you cure the disease that limits them.

Step 1 - BEING vs. BECOMING

For a long time, I truly believed that if someone knew *what* they needed to do, in the order and sequence in which they *needed* to do it, to get the result, then surely they would execute it, right?

Well, under that assumption, *for years*, I provided the tactics *and* strategies.

The formulas *and* templates.

80

The do "this" *and* do "thats."

I even went so far to make it all paint-by-number, so even the rawest beginner could get the desired result.

Year after year, I watched *as* they failed.

I struggled, personally, too.

Because *in* their failure to get the desired result, with me as the *guide*, I knew I had failed, too. Which was not only frustrating. But infuriating. Because, as we know, success is *so* simple.

Solve these *problems*, release the genie:

Problem #1 - They're too scared to *do* hard shit.
Problem #2 - They *don't* stick with it.
Problem #3 - They implemented and executed a *flawed* model from the start.

Consequence of Problem #1 – That person *Never* gets in the game!

Consequence of Problem #2 – FODQ: "The Cycle of Misery," over and over.

Consequence of Problem #3 – Everything works *against* you! – Feeding FODQ!

    1) The Cycle of Staying Small
    2) The Cycle of Missed Opportunities
    3) The Cycle of Mistakes

Once those problems are SOLVED!...

1 – Do Hard Shit

2 – Stick With It

3 – Get The Result

People will ask, **"What's your secret?"**

= You will say, "Here's how I did it - *Go here…*"

= *Get Paid to Become Your Best Self*

<u>*Except*</u>… And this is what I learned:

The character in the story; The person they *are* vs. the person they *want to* become, are two very different people:

> `Information vs. Human Behavior` - A rodeo champion can train us on how how to ride a bull, but he can't take away our fear. A poker champion can teach us how to play cards, but he can't take away our anxiety. A world-class painter can teach us how to paint, but he can't take away our self-doubt. A physical trainer can show us how to achieve fitness, but he can't take away our body-image issues or insecurities. A speech coach can teach us how to present, but he can't take away our nerves. A psychologist can teach us how to deal with trauma, but he can't take away our pain from having no self-worth. And, I can give people ALL the tactics and strategies in the world, but I can't take their *Lesser Self* out of the equation. Hence, *no execution*.

> `YOUR WANT vs. (WHO)YOU ARE` - The reason people under-achieve, get overwhelmed, are frustrated, and feel depressed when it comes to most things in life, especially in the game of entrepreneurship, health, fitness, success, achieving financial security, fulfilment and happiness, is because what they *want* is at odds with *who* they *are*.

TO ACHIEVE THE MEANINGFUL IMPACT WE *WANT* IN LIFE; in our business, in our health and fitness, for our family, and in our relationships, we have to *CHANGE* who we are.

Everybody says, "I *want* to change," to build a better life.

They say, I am "*willing*" to change.

But that part of us that we need to change, the *Lesser Self* that lives inside, never dies without a fight.

Heroic Self vs Lesser Self

This is the real battle:

This is a *battle* of behaviors. This is a *battle* of possibilities. This is a *battle* of conditioned beliefs.

This is a *battle* of pain vs. comfort.

This is a **battle** of stories.

In most of us, our *Lesser Self* is bigger, stronger, smarter, more capable, in better shape, and a far better negotiator.

The Lesser Self doesn't play fair, either.

Your *self-doubts*.

Your *worries*.

Your *fears*.

Your *insecurities*.

Your *lack of confidence*.

Your *past performances* and *old habits*.

Your *tragedies*.

Your *traumas*.

Your *broken upbringing*.

Your *desire* to fit in.

Your *desire for life* to be easier, not as hard.

Your *desire* for comfort.

Your *desire* to "Do it tomorrow."

Every single thing that makes success *harder* and procrastination *easier*, the Lesser Self harnesses, and manipulates, and takes advantage of, in a game of tug-o-war, to defeat your Heroic Self.

Your Heroic Self - is *who* you want to become.

But...

CHANGE IS PAIN

And if you put your hand on a hot burner, causing pain, what is your reflexive response? To remove your hand, *immediately*.

What is our *reflexive response* to almost every kind of pain?

In general, to stop doing whatever is causing it (or will cause that pain).

Change is **PAIN**.

So, when you ask the *Lesser Self* to change, to endure PAIN, what do you imagine his response is?

Abort.

Cease mission.

FUCK YOU!

The truth is, people hate change.

Especially, that *part of us* that we're asking to die, to forever disappear from our life, to leave us alone.

Like a virus, that part of our conscious or unconscious mind, fights to survive.

We may sit around and wish our lives were different, but when the rubber really meets the road, we usually find ourselves wishing we could just hang out in our safe and familiar haunts.

"FAT RYAN"
(Was No Exception)

For 8 years, I allowed that sonofabitch, my *Lesser Self*, to out-smart and outfox me, and to out-negotiate me.

My Heroic Self was weak, small, powerless.

He was *David*.

My Lesser Self was *Goliath*.

The funny thing is, I finally started to see it this way, in that context:

David *vs.* Goliath.

Both of these characters lived inside of me. And both fought, with their voices, as they whispered into my ear, sitting on opposite shoulders, to influence, to persuade, to control my behaviors.

Heroic Self: *(whispered)* Let's get in-shape.

Lesser Self: *(yelled)* Fuck that. Do it tomorrow.

Heroic Self: *(whispered)* Let's eat healthy.

Lesser Self: *(yelled)* Fuck that. You worked hard, you *deserve* a beer.

Heroic Self: *(whispered…)*

Lesser Self: *(yelled)*

Heroic Self: *(whispered…)*

Lesser Self: *(yelled)*

Heroic Self: *(whispered…)*

Lesser Self: *(yelled)*

Needless to say, once I was *aware of* and conscious of this happening. I developed a HATRED for my Lesser Self.

I wanted that motherfucker, dead.

I resented him.

I wanted him *gone*.

He had destroyed my life, for too long.

Step 2 - APPROPRIATE HATRED

From that point forward, I refused to let my Lesser Self win. As soon as I heard his voice trying to negotiate with me. *"You don't need to do it. You can do it tomorrow…"* I silenced him.

Ninety percent (90%) of the battle was *just* recognizing his voice in my head.

That *isn't* me!

That is him.

I started applying this to every aspect of my life.

    Mind.
    Body.
    Business.
    Relationships.

By doing this, the power tables turned:

Lesser Self: *(whispered)* Maybe we can do *it* later.

Heroic Self: *(yelled)* No, we do *it* NOW!

Lesser Self: *(whispered)* I'm tired, I don't really *feel* like it...

Heroic Self: *(yelled)* I don't care if you're tired, GET. OFF. YOUR. ASS!

Lesser Self: *(whispered...)*

Heroic Self: *(**yelled**)*

Lesser Self: *(whispered...)*

Heroic Self: *(**yelled**)*

The best part was? As I transformed myself across Mind, Body, Business, Relationships, I documented my journey. I wrote the stories. I provided the progress updates.

In doing so, I created intellectual property (IP) assets.

I connected with my audience.

I tested message.

I compiled those stories into a book.

My transformation created *demand* for the path I had traveled.

People asked: "How did you do that?"

"What is your secret?"

But more than anything, I discovered this truth:

The Character vs. The Script

The character is the *slave* to the script. The character, in a story, has no free-will. If it's not in the script, he *can't* do it. If it is *in* the script, he must do it. Therefore, the *Author* holds the power.

Inside of StoryAthlete, the *Heroic Self* holds the pen!

What do you want for your life? - (this is the *STORY* you get to write *into* existence):

What are you *sick of* about yourself?

What *attitudes* are sabotaging you?

What *behaviors* are limiting you?

Which of the (3) *negative cycles* are you stuck in and can't escape?

What *bad habits* are not serving you?

What *poor actions* are not getting you closer to your envisioned life?

What negative *addictions* are destroying your progress?

What *Character traits* do you wish you had?

What *Character traits* do you wish you didn't have?

In the face of challenge, how do you *wish* you would respond?

Are you *committing* to do hard shit?

Or, are you *running from* the hard shit that could make you hard(er) to kill?

> **These are the questions I asked myself.** It doesn't matter if it's "Fat Ryan" "Lazy Frank," "Drink-to-much Dan," or "No Discipline Steve." We all have our shit. Even "Paralysis-by-Analysis Heather." And "Doesn't-Ever-Finish George." <u>Not a single person reading this is perfect. Not a single person reading this has reached their (highest) potential</u>. Not a single person reading this doesn't have at least a handful of things they wouldn't love to change about themselves.
>
> > **Real Estate Investing** – Are you living life with the freedom of a full-time real estate investor? If not, why not? What is preventing this? <u>What decisions, behaviors, bad habits, fears, worries, concerns, or limiting beliefs, etc., is holding your Character back from realizing this possibility</u>?
> >
> > > **Marketing Systems** – We all know a well-built marketing system (resulting in lots of customers, clients, users, members, i.e., Deal Flow) is the path to a high income and the financial freedom to say "Fuck you" to any opportunity or headache that doesn't serve your happiness. So, have you built for yourself this kind of system? If not, why not? <u>What decisions, behaviors, bad habits, fears, worries, concerns, or limiting beliefs, etc., is holding your Character back from building such a system or partnering with someone who already has</u>?

Fitness & health – We all agree, without our health, and the health of our loved ones, nothing else matters. So, are you prioritizing your health and fitness, and prioritizing your mission to inspire your loved ones to prioritize theirs? If not, why not? <u>What decisions, behaviors, bad habits, fears, worries, concerns, limiting beliefs, etc., is holding your Character back from getting in peak physical shape, and inspiring your loved ones to prioritize health and fitness, too?</u>

Could be a better parent? – "Fat Ryan," and "All-Business Fletcher," I had to confess: Was a mediocre father at best. The most important job I have in this world, and my rating? *Mediocre!* Was that my intent? No. But mediocre, due to a lot of wrong priorities and poorly designed business systems, i.e., no leverage, etc., rendered me with too little time to best serve my kids. Or myself. Maybe you're in the same boat. If you are, why? <u>What decisions, behaviors, bad habits, fears, worries, concerns, limiting beliefs, etc., is holding your Character back from becoming the greatest parent on earth?</u>

Could be a better spouse? – Entrepreneurs, the 5% of us with the most ambition, often joke about our spouses being saints for putting up with us. But, are we really joking? And, we must confront the truth, is it really funny? For a lot of years, thanks to "Fat Ryan," and "All-Business Fletcher," my wife got to enjoy what was left of me, what little I had left to give, after 12 or 14-hour workdays. I finally had to stop the jokes, and admit, she deserved better. Maybe you're in the same boat. If so, why? <u>What decisions, behaviors, bad habits, fears, worries, concerns, limiting beliefs, etc., is holding your Character back from becoming the greatest spouse on earth?</u>

A good Partner can give you all of the tools and resources, systems and processes, templates and information, and data, you could possibly need to make you successful. <u>But no Partner, no matter how good, can make you look at yourself in the mirror. To honestly evaluate, where your *Lesser Self* is sabotaging you?</u>

As the author of your character's *Script,* that is your *job.*

You hold the pen.

So, as your *Heroic Self*, write the fucking script.

Step 3 – <u>Edit</u> Defective "Genes"

This is the fun part, my friend.

This is the part where you get to punish the *Lesser Self*, for all the pain and suffering he's caused you over the years.

This is the part where you *get* revenge.

Heroic Self = Author

Lesser Self = The Character

Inside the *script* you write, the character has no free-will.

He must obey.

He is a *slave* to what the script reads.

<u>This is how you shift the influence and power *in favor of* the Heroic Self, to finally defeat the Lesser Self.</u>

> **Editing Defective "Genes"** - In a minute, I'll share those (7) defective genes that if replaced with a superior gene, a person automatically gravitates toward *their* potential, no longer stuck in the *Cycle of Misery*.
>
>> **The Destruction of "Fat Ryan"** - I want to repeat, this process hasn't *just* worked for "Fat Ryan. It works for any Lesser Self that needs to be defeated. By holding the pen, literally, and writing the Script, your Heroic Self renders your Lesser Self powerless.
>>
>>> **The Lesson I Shared On This Topic** - What follows is the literal demonstration of how I (and StoryAthletes) use this concept of *Character vs. Script* to chase our highest potential across Mind, Body, Business, Relationships, predictably transforming ourselves to create **demand** for path we traveled. People ask. "How did you do it?" "What is your secret?" And truth is, the secret is really simple:
>>>
>>>> 1) I did hard shit,
>>>> 2) I stuck with it,
>>>> And 3) I *transformed* because of it…

"Ryan" (The Character) Doesn't Get A Say!

(Publish in 2018)

I haven't seen 207lbs on a scale since before Jackson was born. That was 8 years ago. When Mel got pregnant, that's when I started building my Dad-bod.

After just 19 Workouts, I'm down nearly 30lbs. But more important, I feel a million times better.

It apparently shows too, as Ryan France sent me an email the other day, after I had provided an update:

> "Your email yesterday was one of the few that I've actually felt compelled to print out so that I can revisit it time and again. Good stuff. Thanks for continuing to share the journey. I have to say too, I noticed the weight loss in your recent videos. You're looking good - a lot healthier. I can't think of "low energy" without thinking of Jeb. No way you want to be lumped in with that guy."

No, I definitely do not. But looking back, that's about how I felt.

Like Jeb Bush. Like a turd.

Which gets me to a comment from Jay Lieberman yesterday. He bought the same $12 book off Amazon, that I did, that I've been using as my person trainer.

"So, should I be scared to open this thing or what?"

I replied, "No, you shouldn't have any reaction to it. You should be totally unemotional." You don't get to like it. Or dislike it. Because you don't get a choice. It's just the next one in line.

I went on to say, I sometimes ask Mel, "Want to work out with me?" She says, "What's the workout?" I say, don't know. Don't care. Whatever #19 is. It starts in 10 minutes.

You see –

I decided something (19 workouts ago), roughly two months ago. Which is - Ryan is the *Character* in the story I am writing.

And Ryan's *Life* –

Me being the *writer*, Ryan *being* the Character - I have full control over him.

Ryan *doesn't* get a say.

<u>Whatever is in the *script* is what the Character - Ryan - has to do</u>. So, two months ago, I wrote into the script what Ryan is going to do.

"Ryan, the character, is going to get off his fat ass. And he is going to push himself physically, at least 12-minutes a day, in accord to that $12 book he purchased, earlier that week, off of Amazon."

<u>It doesn't matter if Ryan likes it or not. Because Ryan has no power to make decisions</u> - he is merely the Character in the story I am writing.

And that story, is Ryan's Life.

Jay responded back:

"Love the approach."

So, do I. Because it eliminates all the discussion, debate, and negotiation with the Lesser Self, inside one's head, that works to sabotage them, including sabotaged myself for over 8 years.

Now?

Ryan <u>has</u> <u>no</u> <u>choice</u>.

<u>I'm the writer</u>, not Ryan.

Ryan is just the Character. <u>He gets zero say</u>.

<u>He has to behave in the exact way that I wrote the script. And when he gets tired, it's written into the script, that he's to continue to push "as hard as he can, for as long as he can."</u>

Ryan *isn't* allowed to quit.

<u>Ryan has proven for 8 years he isn't capable of making the proper decision about his health and fitness. So, I stepped in, as my Heroic Self, and wrote the script for him, so he no longer has control</u>.

As the writer of your character's *Script* - which determines the outcome of your LIFE - Mind, Body, Business, Relationships - how are you choosing to author it?

<u>MY GREAT EPIPHANY</u>: You are the Writer of your Character's story. You are (also) the Character. If your Character fails, it's because you wrote for your Character a shitty script.

Please! - Read that <u>AGAIN.</u>

91

If you can't, as the *author* of your Story, defeat your *Lesser Self*, then you can't possibly be a good Partner.

Everybody is an expert at telling themselves the "self-defeating" story.

(Lesser Self *dominated*)

From birth, society conditions us to *master* that story.

So, to reverse that and to rewrite the DNA of your Life, you must become equally masterful at telling the "opposite-side" of that story. Not the *Lesser Self* version. But the *Heroic Self* version.

Otherwise, the negative *side* will always win.

Being vs. Becoming

Not, "Who am I?" (currently)

But rather, "Who do I want to become?" (future)

Let's write *that* person into the plotline of your story.

You are the *write*r (of your life's story)

You *control* the Character.

You can give that Character *any* character trait you need him or her to have to be successful.

That *Character* is you.

Thus, who you write about = *Who* you become!!!

The 7 Defective "Genes"

To understand how "gene" editing works, you need to understand how stories govern our results. Thus, if we change our stories, through a chain reaction, we change our results.

It works like this: (Limiting beliefs are the result of our *Lesser Self* stories)

Stories *create* Beliefs

Beliefs *decide* Behaviors

Behaviors *determine* Actions

Actions are what *dictate* our **Results**

Thus, we have the power to *change* our results in Life, by changing the *stories* we tell ourselves.

In the story above, I demonstrated how this worked.

I wrote for my Character a *new* story.

> A new *set* of stories.
>
> *Stories* that empowered my character by eliminating his *Lesser Self* inputs.
>
> By doing this, I *created* the desired Result.

EVERYTHING IS CAUSE AND EFFECT:

So, to re-write the DNA of our Life, we must accept a few facts:

A) The ability *to do so* is *100%* in our control.

B) Our Results (positive or negative) equal the *SUM* of our behaviors.

If our behaviors are *Lesser Self* dominated, then our Life will be *Lesser Self* dominated and so, too, will our Results. Meaning, FODQ – the perpetual Cycle of Misery.

= *Nobody* is inspired by you

= You *never* live up to your potential

If our behaviors are *Heroic Self* dominated, then our Life will be *Heroic Self* dominated and so, too, will our Results. Meaning, 1) Did hard shit, 2) Stuck with it. And 3) Got the transformative Result...

= People *are* inspired by you

= They will ask, **"How?... What is your secret?"**

= You say, "Here's how I did it – *Go here...*"

= *Get Paid To Become Your Best Self*

C) Your *Lesser Self* is your only true enemy!

As your Partner, I could give you every tool, resource, system, funnel process, etc., you need to *be* successful. But if you don't erase the *Lesser Self* from your Character script, your *Lesser Self* will sabotage every advantage provided.

"Genes" Equal Behaviors

In the opening if this book, I wrote, "If you want to change your world, you have to change how you see it."

Specifically, I wrote this paragraph:

```
From this point forward, we shall see your life
as a string of DNA. To improve your DNA, we
must knock out defective genes. And knock-in
new superior genes. (Keep reading, there are 7
"gene sequences" that cause people to never
live up to their potential in life. Should we
replace these "gene sequences," with new
superior "gene sequences", our potential gets
achieved.)
```

In the context of everything we have discussed so far, there are (7) gene sequences that keep people from living up to their potential.

(7) gene sequences - that **keep** people *stunted*.

That **keep** people - *limited*.

GENE EDITING: Instead of *being* Lesser Self dominated, we *become* Heroic Self dominated:

Heroic Self - (**Behavior**)	Versus	Lesser Self - (**Behavior**)
superior "gene"	**replacing**	defective "gene"
DECISION	replaces	INDECISION
COMMITMENT	replaces	NO COMMITMENT
DISCIPLINE	replaces	NO DISCPLINE
SUSTAINED DISCIPLINE	replaces	SUSTAINED EXCUSES
GRIT	replaces	NO GRIT
PERSISTENCE	replaces	NO PERSITENCE
NEVER QUITS	replaces	ALWAYS QUITS
Documents the Journey	(THE RESULTS)	No Journey to Document
Shares The Lessons		Nothing To Share
Becomes the Pace Car		Finishes Last
= Inspires Others!	(THE TRUTH)	**= Inspires No One!**

Becoming successful in any endeavor, especially when provided with a *proper* model from the start, truly *is* this simple.

Living 'The StoryAthlete Way'

Story + Athlete = *Story*Athlete

    Story = The Sport

    Athlete = Elite Performance

It works like this:

If we change the *stories* we write for our Character, we change our character's *Results*!

    Stories *create* Beliefs

        Beliefs *decide* Behaviors

            Behaviors *determine* Actions

                Actions are what *dictate* our **Results**

Through our ability to write the character *Script*, we choose to write the *STORY* we want to live *into* existence.

This is how we live the LIFE of our *Heroic Self*.

Your Heroic Self would *make* for a good Partner.

Your *Lesser Self*?

We have no interest in that motherfucker. (Appropriate Hatred)

As a community of StoryAthletes, driven by our *Heroic Self*, it should be no wonder how we experience transformation:

It should be no wonder *how* we operate as full-time real estate investors.

It should be no wonder *how* we build profitable online businesses.

It should be no wonder *how* we achieve peak energy and physical fitness.

It should be no wonder *how* we develop ourselves into compelling storytellers.

It should be no wonder *how* we lead philanthropic movements.

It should be no wonder *how* we turn our *LIFE* into our business.

It should be no wonder *how* we get *PAID* to become our best self.

The *Path* is as simple as this:

A) We write the character *Script* the way it needs to be written – *Period!*

    a. (Defeats Lesser Self)

B) We don't execute or implement *flawed* models from the start

    a. (Defeats the *trio* of negative cycles)

C) We don't fall *prey* to FODQ; the Cycle of Misery

    a. (= Sustained progress)

        i. The End Result (of this 1% Journey)

            1. Do Hard Shit

            2. Stick With It

            3. Get The (Transformative) Result

It goes back to *these* 15 words:

"Everything you want in life can be had, *IF…* you *just* stop quitting on yourself."

TRUTH #5
1% Daily Gains, Compounded (= 37X Growth)

Poor people are always fascinated *with* instant growth.

Fast progress and *instant* gratification.

Which is interesting because they are the same people *who continue* to be poor, having never found "the magic bullet" they are searching for.

Secrets.

Shortcuts.

Loopholes.

They search and search but never find them.

Meanwhile, successful people simply *focus* on the Science of 1% Daily Improvement.

Step 1 – A Proper Expectation

Bill Gates has said:

"Most people overestimate what they can do in one year and underestimate what they can do in ten years."

By far, the biggest reason for why people succumb to the Cycle of Misery, FODQ, then repeat that journey many times over, for years, is because of they have an *improper* expectation from the start.

Everybody thinks *it* should be easier.

Everybody thinks *it* should happen faster.

(That is not *the* reality)

But *that* is what they believe.

So, when that overestimated-progress doesn't happen as fast, or isn't as easy as they expect, people feel like failures. And that *FEAR* of failure, influences them to *abandon* their original designed path.

Which, by the way, may have been a *proper* path.

How frustrating, right?

After two weeks of being lost in the woods, you were just 2 miles from hitting the main road where someone could have rescued you. But, you thought that road should've been there sooner, so you turned back.

This deviation from the *proper* path, based on an *"improper* expectation," leads you back into the woods.

There – you DIE.

This is what happens to entrepreneurs.

"Most people overestimate what they can do in one year and underestimate what they can do in ten years."

This is why A Proper Expectation, about every aspect of the journey that lies ahead; Mind, Body, Business, Relationships, is the needed mindset for turning your LIFE into your business.

A Proper Expectation is what combats the *FEAR* of Failure…

A Proper Expectation is what combats the *FEAR* of *"What if…I'm on the wrong path?!"*

The Dominant Enemy

That **FEAR** is what the *Lesser Self* feeds on:

"What if…"

"What if…"

"What if…"

And it's that psychological nightmare that the *Lesser Self* constructs, that sabotages the direction of a good compass.

I don't want to look like a *failure* to my family.

I don't want to look like *a failure* to my friends.

I don't want to look like a *failure* in the mirror.

"I know, I should be *there* by now," we say to ourselves.

"It shouldn't *take* this long."

"It shouldn't be *this* hard."

Maybe I doing it *wrong*?

I must be *going* in the wrong direction.

Shift course.

Pivot direction.

Turn Back? – (frustration, overwhelm, depression…)

Quit.

Start Over.

It is this *psychological* chain-of-events, kicked off by that *first* improper expectation, created by the Lesser Self, *fueled* by the FEAR of failure, that keeps people from moving forward on that hard *but* proper path.

So, let's combat that **dominant** enemy:

Fear of Failure → *Fuels* the Lesser Self → *Creates* an Improper Expectation

DOMINANT ENEMY = FEAR OF FAILURE. Right here, right now, I want to cure you of this fear so the *Lesser Self* can't use it (against you) to construct psychological nightmares.

> **First, and foremost, WE ARE SCIENTISTS** - Scientists do not experience failure. They test variables through *THE* experimentation process, not knowing or caring about the outcome. They are after *data*. That data is then used to formulate a new hypothesis to run another experiment. From that experiment, more data gets collected. This process repeats. In 1894, the first U.S. Polio Epidemic occurred. It took 11-years to identify the contagious nature of the disease. It took another 3-years to detect the virus itself. And it wasn't until 1935 that the first vaccine trials started. In 1944, a full 48 years after the first U.S. Epidemic, FDR claimed victory over Polio. Said differently, in a context outside of science, after "48 years of failure," success finally happened. In reality, no failure happened because scientists and researchers don't fail. They learn. They collect data. They test more variables. Using that data, they design better experiments, with more promising outcomes. The idea of Failure, and the *fear* of it, is purely a Mind-created false-understanding of how success happens.
>
> > **FAILURE IS NOT REAL, DATA IS** - Every day, every minute, every decision is an experiment that you execute in the Lab of Life. Failure is not real. Data is. So, from this data, what did you learn? People who learn to be researchers in the Lab of Life, testing on themselves, learn to separate the experiment and outcome from their identity and emotions. I live my life to collect data. From that data, positive or negative it doesn't matter, I can better design the next experiment. So what if it takes one or two years, or 48 years, to discover my Life's Breakthrough. I'm here to play the game that I love. Winning the Super Bowl is the icing on top. If Tom Brady played on a different team, without all the dozens of little factors that contributed to the *whole* of the New England Patriots. There is no way he, nor the Patriots, ever achieve what they did. In science, in the Lab, you can have 48 correct variables, but it only takes one wrong variable to destroy the entire outcome. Life and success are a fucking Rubik's Cube, every time you twist it; you screw up the other side. The secret to solving a Rubik's Cube is to learn the cause-and-effect relationship. Every twist of the cube is a mini experiment that gives you data. Data is real. Failure is not. You may have to make 75 wrong moves to learn the data to be able to make the next 75 right moves.
> >
> > > **"FEAR OF FAILURE" IS A FUCKING GHOST** - When I was maybe seven or eight years old, I was terrified of the monsters in the dark. One night, at my cousin's house, we watched "The Night of the Living Dead." I had nightmares for weeks. My parents assured me, "Movies aren't real." "Zombies aren't real." "There is nothing to be afraid of." That didn't help me, though. I still snuck into their bedroom at night, with my pillow and blanket, and made a bed and slept

on their floor. Desperate to help me. My mom even made me "Monster Spray," by brewing a bunch of spices and other ingredients, then bottled it into an aerosol can. Unbeknownst to me, she just wrapped her deodorant can with a "Monster Spray" label. Nonetheless, I believed in it. And for weeks, she loves to tell this story, she could hear me in my room spraying the hell out of those monsters. If this sounds ridiculous, that I used fake Monster Spray, i.e., deodorant, to kill fake Monsters that didn't exist, but felt less scared when I sprayed it, it's because it is. "Failure" is no more real than those monsters and ghosts that I feared when I was eight. My Mom devised a tool to help me. And here, I have devised a tool to help you. Your "Monster Spray" equivalent, is the *identity* of the Researcher. You are a Researcher first, not the Entrepreneur, or anything else. And THE Researcher specializes in the management of *proper* expectation.

PROPER EXPECTATION = 1% DAILY IMPROVEMENT – Goal setting is shit. Stop making goals. I can't tell you how many times people have asked me what my five-year goal is. Each time I tell them I have no damn clue. Because who I am today and then three months from now, and what I'll know then, and be capable of, will be entirely different than what it is today. What I can tell you though is that I'm a slave to my purpose. "To create a movement of movements by helping others to create their own." That is my North Star. I zig and zag, but that purpose keeps me moving forward in a direction that is true. Further, "To inspire the uninspired." That is the mission I must achieve if I plan to succeed in the stated purpose. Movements are forged with inspired people. With this Purpose in place, as my North Star, I can be guided in the 1% journey to achieve it. It may take 48 years. *Who cares!*

Once we realize that failure isn't real, but data is, then FAILURE is no longer something to FEAR. This shift in thinking prevents the psychological chain-of-events from happening, created by the Lesser Self, that destroys our ability to walk the hard *but* proper path.

We should know, by now, the *proper* path is never easy.

It's simple…

But it's not easy…

Step 2 - Harness COMPOUNDING

If you take away nothing else from this book, please take this:

<u>The Science of 1% Daily Improvement</u>

    That's it.

That's all you have to do each day.

Every day, an asset.

    Mind.
    Body.
    Business.
    Relationships.

<u>Albert Einstein has been attributed with saying,</u> *"Compound interest is the 8th wonder of the world."*

    Warren Buffet, our generation's greatest investor, has said. "Life is like a snowball. The important thing is finding wet snow *and* a really long hill." Same sentiment. The power of compounding.

    It's *not* a sprint.

    It's a marathon.

    It's not a race.

    It's the *deliberate* practice of *strategic* patience.

    I first learned about the *Aggregation of Marginal Gains*, the power of traveling *The 1% Journey*, after reading James Clear's book, Atomic Habits, and reading about Dave Brailsford.

    <u>From the book Atomic Habits by James Clear - buy it</u>:

    THE PATH TO ESCAPE MEDIOCRITY - In 2003, the British Cycling organization hired Dave Brailsford as its new performance director. <u>At the time, professional cyclists in Great Britain had endured nearly one hundred years of mediocrity</u>. In fact, the performance of British riders has been so underwhelming that one of the top bike manufacturers in Europe refused to sell bikes to the team because they were afraid that it would hurt sales if other professionals saw the Brits using their gear.

> **THE AGGREGATION OF MARGINAL GAINS** - Brailsford had been hired to put British Cycling on a new trajectory. What made him different from previous coaches was his relentless commitment to strategy that he referred to as "the aggregation of marginal gains," which was the philosophy of searching for a tiny margin of improvement in everything you do. Brailsford said, "The whole principle came from the idea that if you broke down everything you could think of that goes into ride a bike, then improve it by 1%, you will get a significant increase when you put them altogether.
>
> **TRANSFORMATIVE RESULTS** - In just 5 years, after adopting this belief and strategy, at the 2008 Olympics, British cyclists won an astounding 60% of the gold medals available. Setting 9 Olympic records and 7 world records. This is the power of recognizing an inferior approach and committing to long-term, strategic fixes. It takes time. But results can be significant, record-breaking and can come ahead of schedule if you're serious about long-term success.
>
> **WHAT'S THEIR SECRET?** - Nothing complex or sophisticated. Just the Science of 1% daily improvement. Get better each day by 1%, harness compounding, and never miss a day of improvement or gains. Step 1) Do Hard Shit. Step 2) Stick With It. Step 3) Get The Transformative Result.

Fixing mistakes doesn't *typically* happen all at once. To expect immediate transformation would be an improper expectation. Which, we already know the dangers of where that leads.

Poor, unsuccessful, unhappy, unfulfilled people chase *instant* gratification.

Successful people *sustain* 1% daily improvement.

> Challenge-Based-Life!

The 1% Journey - the perpetual *plodding* to achieve (exponential) growth.

> Mind.
> Body.
> Business.
> Relationships.

HABITS ARE THE COMPOUND INTEREST OF SELF-IMPROVEMENT. Sustained Discipline, to stay the course of The 1% Journey, is the most important habit to develop and prioritize.

Every day, 1%, 1%, 1%... = 37X Growth

Step 3 – Exponential Growth

<u>Look around, do most people achieve *their* envisioned life?</u>

Do they have income they want?

Do they have the time-freedom they want?

Do they have the health and fitness they want?

Are they making the impact they want?

Or, do they travel the *Cycle of Misery*, year after year?

If you ask people if they want 37X growth over the next calendar year, every person you ask will answer *yes*.

Hell yes!

<u>Except, here's the problem</u>: To get 37X growth, you have to be *committed* to 1% daily gains. Which, in the beginning, *feels* like no progress at all. To demonstrate this, take the doubling of a penny.

Day 1 – start with 1 penny.

Day 2 – double it = 2 pennies

Day 3 – double it = 4 pennies

Day 4 – doubling continues = 8 pennies

Day 5 = 16 pennies

Day 6 = 32 pennies

Day 7 = 64 pennies

<u>If you had to work your ass off for 7-days straight, to earn 64 pennies, would you be interested in continuing?</u>

After all, 64 pennies isn't even one dollar.

So, most people quit.

Fuck that, *too much work*.

Lesser Self, *"There has to be an easier way."*

So, boom!

The Cycle of Misery already *starts* over.

FODQ

Some people *persist*, though:

Day 8 = 128 pennies

Day 9 = 256 pennies

Day 10 = 512 pennies

Day 11 = 1024 pennies

Day 12 = 2048 pennies

Day 13 = 4096 pennies

Day 14 = 8192 pennies

If you had to work your ass off for 14-days straight, to earn 8,192 pennies, would you be interested in continuing?

Said different, would you work your ass off, 2-weeks straight, for $81.92

It's not easy to get 1% better every day!

You have to *fight* for it.

You have to show up.

You have to put in the work.

Mind.
Body.
Business.
Relationships.

The answer is, *No*, most people aren't willing to bust their ass for 2-weeks straight, with no days off, to earn a measly eighty-one bucks.

So, *again*, they quit.

Lesser Self, *"There has to be an easier way."*

So, boom!

The Cycle of Misery *starts* again.

FODQ

The *committed* though, continue: (compounding, 1%, 1%, 1%, starts to pay off)

Day 15 = 16,392 pennies

Day 16 = 32,748 pennies

Day 17 = 65,568 pennies

Day 18 = 131,136 pennies

Day 19 = 262,272 pennies

Day 20 = 524,544 pennies

Day 21 = 1,049,088 pennies

If you had to work your ass off for 21-days straight, to earn 1,049,088 pennies, would you be interested in continuing?

Do that math.

That's $10,490.88.

Hell yeah, most people would be *interested* in busting their ass for 3-weeks straight, no days off, to make ten-thousand bucks.

Except, here is the problem.

COMMITED vs. INTERESTED.

Everyone is *interested* in 37X growth.

But not everyone is *committed* to fight for 1% daily gains.

By the way, at the end of 30-days, by doubling that penny every day for a month, the committed person, who persists, doesn't quit, stays the course, by *defeating* his Lesser Self, collects $1.3 million.

Committed people (*not* interested people) achieve Exponential Growth!

The beautiful part, when it comes to the Science of 1% Daily Improvement – Compounding - can be applied to Skill Acquisition AND Execution. Which is what creates *exponential* success.

Slow, at first.

Painfully slow, at first.

But then, "*Overnight*" success!

At least, that's what it looks like. Because, for months or years, progress is painfully slow, but then – boom! – compounding *is* harnessed. And our *transformative* result accelerates like a rocket.

Ask *real* entrepreneurs.

There is no *such thing* as an "overnight success."

They have been honing their sills, *1% daily* improvement, for years.

No days off.

They just keep showing up.

Let me tell you a story that solidifies this point; our *ability* to choose, to experience exponential growth.

Committed vs. Interested?

It's *easy* to be interested.

It's quite another, to *be* committed.

You can apply the Science of *1% daily improvement*, to anything, to achieve the transformative result.

```
My good friend Patrick Bove, one hell of copywriter at Agora,
tagged me in a post the other day. He was addressing the question
he gets several times per week.

Which is:

"What's the fastest way to get good at copywriting?"
```

Keep in mind, people ask that same question about everything:

-- "What's the fastest way to lose 20-pounds?"

-- "What's the fastest way to become a full-time RE investor?"

-- "What the fastest way to become a good content creator?"

-- "What's the fastest way to turn $100 into $2 million?"

He (Patrick) answered:

"Each time - my answer is the same: **There are no shortcuts**. It takes years for even the most promising junior [copywriter] to become dangerous. I've met ONE exception to the rule... Ryan Fletcher. And I don't expect to find another like him anytime soon."

Back when I was a copywriter at Agora, too, where I met Patrick, I was often asked the same question. Some version of "What's your secret?" Like "How did you get so good so fast?" In other words, "I want to be as good as you, but I'm not. So, what am I missing?"

Each time - like Patrick - my answer was the same:

"I have more binders than you."

That's it.

That's my secret. I read more books. I studied more packages. I collected more templates. I organized more of that research into a binder system so that I could actually use it - not just collect it…

"I have more binders than you."

But really, it comes down to something simpler. Commitment. When I make a commitment, I'm committed. I wasn't "interested" in becoming a good copywriter, as Patrick pointed out. I was committed to it. That commitment then mapped to my behaviors.

"I have more binders than you."

Is simply the visual demonstration of that commitment.

People ask me, "How in the hell did you build ImpactClub®?" More than $2 million now donated to local charities. Same answer. I was *committed* to building it. I wasn't "interested" in building it. I was *committed*, and every day, I strived to get just 1% more built...

For the record, though, ImpactClub® isn't built. It's barely in its infancy. It's a child. It's a baby.

When we're donating over $100 mil per quarter, $400 million annually, then I'll consider it *built*. Where we're at right now, though, that's *just* a good start.

But it isn't built!

Which gets to the difference: **"Committed vs. Interested."**

People who are *interested*, see an outcome and just want it. Immediate. Instant gratification. Whereas, the person who is *committed*, imagines an outcome that is far bigger than he can see right now, then *commits* to getting *just 1% closer* each day. Even if it takes years.

Now apply this to "The Journey" of *becoming* your very best self. Assuming there was NO Compounding, 1% daily improvement would equal a 365% better you at the end of one calendar year.

But *Compounding* does exist, so in reality, that's a 37X better you.

Mind.
Body.
Business.
Relationships

The Result: 37X growth

Everyone - is *interested* in that.

But, *daily*, 1% growth?

Only the most committed make *that* their priority. Which is why only the *committed* experience 3700% growth.

It takes an extremely *disciplined*…

And dedicated person, to *purposely* strive for 1% daily improvement.

"I have more binders than you" - compiled *one*-page at a time.

Thankfully, the Partners we surround ourselves with inside of *Story*Athlete, are those kinds of people.

Committed, not just interested…

Step 1 – Do Hard Shit - (by living the *Challenge-based Life + 1%* Journey)

Step 2 – Stick With It – (*defeats* the Lesser Self *and* the Cycle of Misery; FODQ)

Step 3 – Get The Result – (Achieves *and* Inspires)

People will ask, **"What's your secret?"**

= You will say, "Here's how I did it - *Go here...*"

= *Get Paid to Become Your Best Self*

CHECKPOINT:

<u>On the surface, everything in this book you have read makes sense to you. You get it. You understand the path. But what is the *likelihood* that you will execute it on your own?</u>

I know everybody has good intentions.

I had good intentions, *too.*

I'm going to do *this.*

This time, I *finally* understand the path.

This time, no quitting on myself.

Trust me, I know how this shit plays out. Our good intentions are noble. They're a start. But our intentions *won't* carry us through to the finish line. To achieve that, we need to be pushed by teammates.

<u>Entrepreneurs, elite athletes, high achievers - immediately understand this:</u>

Alone we are weak - (the *Lesser Self* doesn't like to admit this)

Together, we are strong – (the Heroic Self *knows* this)

We *will* quit on ourselves.

But, we *won't* quit on our teammates.

TRUTH #6
Open Source = Shared *Partner* Breakthroughs

Everybody thinks that they can do it by themselves, or that support is the last piece of the equation.

That - is the *myth.*

That is the Lie.

Support and "Open Source" are the WRECKING-BALLS that break down the wall to growth.

Write this down: "Open-Source Movement."

What is it?

How does it work?

Step 1 – Notice The Trend

In industry after industry, there is *disruption* happening. Netflix replaced Blockbuster. Digital cameras replaced Kodak. iPhones replaced digital cameras. Uber replaced taxis.

Expedia replaced travel agents.

Amazon killed off bookstores.

Amazon is killing off retail.

Etc.

Some say it is "software and technology" that is disrupting these industries. But it is not. Because technology is *just* a tool, like a hammer.

A *tool* must be used.

A tool can be effective, *yes*, but a tool cannot *do* anything by itself.

To be effective, a tool must be used – (by someone)

And, to disrupt an industry, it must be innovated upon – (by someone)

So, while everyone says that, "Technology and software is causing disruption."

It is not.

It's the people that are operating in a collaborative process *behind* the technology, that is driving *these* technologies forward, **that are *disrupting* industries, due to *shared* breakthroughs.**

You (ALONE) vs. Us (TOGETHER)

To really understand the competitive *difference* of operating in an Open Source versus operating alone, you should quickly revisit the three (3) negative cycles that feed the Cycle of Misery: *FODQ*...

<u>The Cycle of Staying Small</u>

    a) **Problem**: No prioritization on Asset creation, i.e. No leverage
    b) **Result**: Runs out of time

<u>The Cycle of Missed Opportunities</u>

    a) **Problem**: Not enough skill, resources, or access to connections
    b) **Result**: Lacks enough confidence to execute

<u>The Cycle of Mistakes</u>

    a) **Problem**: The dangers of not knowing *what* you don't know
    b) **Result**: Steps into too much Risk

At the same time, this entrepreneur is trying to hold his *Lesser Self* at bay, so that the psychological chain-of-events doesn't occur, that creates the *improper* expectation that sabotages a proper path.

One misstep, one lapse in mental toughness = FODQ *like* dominos...

The Less Self takes control:

Delay.

Procrastination.

Paralysis-by-analysis.

Second-guessing.

Self-doubt.

Frustration...

<u>We know how *prominent* this cycle is</u>.

And, when you operate alone, these are all the challenges that you must face by yourself and alone.

111

In the typical entrepreneur world, it goes like this:

Entrepreneur A, works on Project A.

Entrepreneur B, works on Project B

Entrepreneur C, works on Project C.

Where Projects A, B, and C, are usually their own projects, and are all being built alone, by that entrepreneur, and usually, he has limited-time, limited-funding, and limited resources.

Which leads to painfully slow progress.

Frustration… ODQ

And virtually no new innovation.

You can't fault him for fighting hard and doing his best, but in the end, the cards are stacked against him.

To escape this, you step *into* the Open Source:

Step 2 - Shared Breakthroughs

Speed-of-innovation is what entrepreneurial *success* is built on. *Who* can get the data from experimentation the fastest? And *who* can use that data, due to shared breakthroughs, to innovate faster?

This is why Startup Accelerator programs (YCombinator, etc.) exist…

To *share* breakthroughs.

This is why Elon Musk decided to make ALL of Tesla's patents, public:

> **OPEN-SOURCE MOVEMENT** - Back in 2014, Elon Musk made Tesla's patents available for anyone to use for free, stating: "Yesterday, there was a wall of Tesla patents in the lobby of our Palo Alto headquarters. That is no longer the case. They have been removed, in the spirit of the open source movement, for the advancement of electric vehicle technology. Tesla Motors was created to accelerate the advent of sustainable transport. If we clear a path to the creation of compelling electric vehicles, but then lay intellectual property landmines behind us to inhibit others, we are acting in a manner contrary to that goal. Tesla will not initiate patent lawsuits against anyone who, in good faith, wants to use our technology.

> **COLLABORATIVE PROCESS: THE BEST MINDS** - Technology leadership is not defined by patents, which history has repeatedly shown to be small protection indeed against a determined competitor, <u>but rather by the ability of a company to attract and motivate the world's most talented engineers</u>. We believe that applying the open-source philosophy to our patents will strengthen rather than diminish Tesla's position in this regard.
>
> **SHARED BREAKTRHOUGHS** - We believe that Tesla, other companies making electric cars, and the world would all benefit from a common, rapidly-evolving technology platform.

Elon did this because he knew he needed more *minds* collaborating together, to drive the central project forward.

<u>Open Source, different than operating alone, works like this:</u>

Entrepreneur A, works to improve **Project D**

Entrepreneur B, works to improve **Project D**

Entrepreneur C, works to improve **Project D**

Where Project D is a central framework, set of tools, or system, that each person within the Community can add to, change, and or borrow from to rapidly advance innovation. <u>Never does a contributor, have to start from scratch, but rather, they can start on the foundation of innovation that's already been created</u>.

Experimentation happens, faster.

Data is created, faster.

Breakthroughs are discovered, faster.

These breakthroughs get *shared* with the Open-Source Community.

Innovation, *at* light speed.

Progress is rapid.

Excitement *vs. frustration*.

FOR OBVIOUS REASONS: Open-Source Communities are becoming the great new advantage of the ambitious entrepreneur. NOT: Where can I find information to learn about X? But rather, how I can access a Community that is FOCUSED on Advancing X, through SHARED breakthroughs?

Step 3 – The Most Committed

Committed *vs. Interested*.

Trust me!

You don't want "interested" people, who want things but aren't committed, to drag down the collective brain power.

Givers *vs. Takers*.

True Players *vs. Water boys*.

Midway through this book, I asked you the question: (under Truth #4)

WHAT ARE YOU WILLING TO SACRIFICE?

This is the question that every great coach, player, teammate, asks of one another and of themselves. Because building a strong *Open Source* is no different than building a championship team.

What are you willing to sacrifice?

What are you willing to commit to?

Same question.

Inside of StoryAthlete, there are 6 Foundations that force growth:

Talking About It vs. Doing It – We have talked about how to write the character Script, to defeat the Lesser self. Genetic Engineering, CRISPR; to replace the 7 defective behaviors with superior behaviors. Also, the 1% Journey; committed vs. interested, to achieve 37X growth. And, about FODQ, the Cycle of Misery; and how to defeat it by eliminating the three (3) negative cycles that feed it. Talking about it, though, won't create transformation. Knowing something and executing something are two *very* different things. So, what is the behavioral infrastructure that forces growth, through teammate and Partner accountability?

Remember, the formula to *success* is so simple:

1 – Do Hard Shit

2 – Stick With It

3 – Get the *Transformative* Result

So, what are the 6 foundations, that FORCE growth?

Because, although...

1) <u>We can show any *Partner* how to become a full-time real estate investor:</u>

   a) By giving unlimited *access to all* of our systems, processes, and protocols...

   b) By answering *any* and all of their questions.

   c) And by sharing *all* of our future breakthroughs.

2) <u>AND, show them how to build an *ultra*-profitable online business:</u>

   a) By giving unlimited *access to all* of our systems, processes, and protocols...

   b) By answering *any* and all of their questions.

   c) And by sharing *all* of our future breakthroughs.

3) <u>AND, show them how to live *in* peak energy and *be* in peak physical fitness:</u>

   a) By giving unlimited *access to all* of our systems, processes, and protocols...

   b) By answering *any* and all of their questions.

   c) And by sharing *all* of our future breakthroughs.

4) <u>AND, show them how to lead a *movement*, donating thousands to local charities:</u>

   a) By giving unlimited *access to all* of our systems, processes, and protocols...

   b) By answering *any* and all of their questions.

   c) And by sharing *all* of our future breakthroughs.

5) <u>AND, show them how to tell *Stories* to build an audience of *1000 True Fans:*</u>

   a) By giving unlimited *access to all* of our systems, processes, and protocols...

   b) By answering *any* and all of their questions.

   d) And by sharing *all* of our future breakthroughs.

<u>We can't **make them** execute it.</u>

So, to FORCE the most development out of every Partner inside the Open Source, we have identified the six (6) required foundations *that create* elevated *GRIT-*levels in a person.

If you have never read Angela Duckworth's book, *GRIT*, I highly recommend that you read it. But the essence of the entire book states, all 200+ pages, can be summarized, just like this:

A person with GRIT - doesn't quit.

And a person with GRIT - isn't afraid to do hard shit.

The primary objective of StoryAthlete?

Hard(er) to kill; mentally, physically, financially.

Mind.
Body.
Business.

So, that we can powerfully *serve* the **Relationships** in our life!

As a *stronger* financial provider

As a *superior* parent

As a more *present* spouse

As a *better* sibling

Or, as a more *capable* friend or family member

Here are the 6 Foundations that FORCE growth: (Heroic Self vs. Lesser Self)

After reading hundreds of books on elite athletes, and entrepreneurs, and CEOs. About founders and competitors who get to the peak of their sport or industry, I have learned one thing:

They don't leave "growth" to chance.

They design an *operating system*, a framework, to force it:

By designing such a framework, a kind of decision-making infrastructure if you will, their decisions, of their Heroic Self, are already cemented into the Character *Script*, so there is no indecision.

Foundation #1: Default-YES vs. Default-NO - This is a mindset. The Lesser Self is dominated by the Default-NO mindset. "It's too hard." "Oh, I could never do that." "I wish I could do that, but..." "I'm not athletic." "I'm not good enough." "I'm not smart enough." "Right now, I don't have enough time." Etc. You get the point. Where the Heroic Self, with a Default-YES mindset, commits, then figures it out later. Last year, as a Community, we committed to run a Spartan Trifecta. At least half the StoryAthletes who committed to run the Trifecta had never even run a 5K before their commitment. Who cares! They'll figure it out! Those, with elevated levels of GRIT, don't just talk about living a Challenge-based Life. They actually live it. They "Embrace The Suck." After only 20 days of the 100 Burpee Regimen, because it was so transformational, not physically, but mentally, emotionally, several committed to sustaining the 100 Burpee Regimen each day for life. Oh my god, that sounds terrible. Yep. It's called GRIT. The funny thing is, as you sustain your commitment, that pain soon turns to pleasure. Default-YES. Give me more. Former athletes will recall the pain of, and be reminded of, how good it made them feel, after a suffering workout. "That sucked. But damn, it felt good." For entrepreneurs, this equates to being able to solve massively-complex-problems under pressure and stress. "That sucked. But damn, it felt good." This mindset; Defeat-YES toward doing hard shit, forces us to expand our limits. We're never going to be ready. There is never going to be a perfect time. It's always going to be hard. Never going to be easy. There is always going to be roadblocks and obstacles. Nothing is going to go as planned. Everything is bound to go wrong. In the words of Jocko, "Good!" Default-YES. Bring it on. Let's see what you can throw at me. First, we commit. Then we figure it out.

#2 - Intensity vs. Checking the Box - Step 1, Default-YES - Do hard shit. Check. Now, understand. The journey we have chosen is about getting a transformative result. Not comfort. Transformation doesn't happen because someone goes to the gym. Just look at the majority of the people at the gym. They're all out of shape, on elliptical machines, reading *Us Weekly*, as they pretend to push themselves. Now, walk over to a CrossFit gym or go run a Spartan Race, and you'll find people who appear to be superhuman. Fucken abs on top of abs on top of abs. Flying through the air like a dolphin on a bar. Doing kipping pull-ups and Olympic lifts. Doing wall balls and burpees until they almost pass out. If you can listen to headphones while you work out, then you aren't practicing Intensity. Intensity is what tells the brain, "Hey, we're fucking dying here. Help us." Because of that signal, the brain triggers the release of growth hormone. Growth hormone burns fat and builds muscle. I highly recommend you read the book, "Learning to Breathe Fire," about the Rise of CrossFit. The StoryAthlete-GRIT Regimen is rooted in Intensity. Will it hurt? You bet your ass. Will it transform you? Absolutely. For the record, I have never seen a badass on an elliptical machine. I know, "they're better for your knees." "Lower impact, more comfortable." Etc. Fuck comfort, though. Comfort is the home of the Lesser Self. Fitness, by the way, is just metaphor. Deliberate intensity, not just checking the box, gets applied to business and relationships, too. Don't just show up. Compete with yourself. Go hard. Choosing intensity proves to yourself that you are capable of more. Lesser Self wants comfort. Heroic Self deliberately chooses pain ;-).

#3 - Suffer Together vs. Suffer Alone - This is pretty simple. When you're alone, and shit starts to suck, and get painful, you quit. The Lesser Self has no issues or qualms whatsoever about quitting on himself. The Heroic Self though, doesn't suffer or *endure* the assigned pain for his good. He does it to be "the rock" to those he's suffering alongside. I have heard Navy SEALs say, "I don't fight for me. I fight for my brother to the left and the right of me." Suffering alone is damn near impossible. Suffering, with others? Well, "Those who suffer together, bond together." It's these friendships, and the social contract that gets created, "I won't quit on you. You won't quit on me," that leads StoryAthletes to earn elevated-levels-of-GRIT as become their true Heroic Self.

#4 - GO, NO-GO vs. Random Check-ins - The science of 1% daily improvement. Compounding! Doesn't take days off. Achieving exponential growth is about sustained 1% gains. Not a week on. Then a week off. To every StoryAthlete that commits to the GRIT protocol, it's made clear; if they miss one day, failing to post their required assignment by the deadline, they get booted from their assigned Team. You want to check-in randomly and sporadically, and only do the GRIT protocol when it is convenient for you? "Good!" Then do it by yourself without a team because clearly, you're not a good teammate. "Go, No-Go." Each day is pass or fail. If you fail, you get to go home and get that warm bowl of soup and hot a chocolate. Meanwhile, your teammates will continue to suffer, by choice, because they have developed the elevated GRIT levels to do so. "It's not convenient." "I didn't have time." "I was traveling." "I forgot." None of that shit flies. GRIT is about commitment, not convenience. Through previous rounds of GRIT, we have witnessed incredible 'Tests of Will,' completed in hotel rooms, airports. In office meeting spaces. On the beach. Even in a hospital emergency room. Your Team, as a Partner who is counting on you, doesn't give a shit how you get it done. Just get it done. But if it's a true emergency and you need help, reach out. And they will all be lined up to support you. Life happens. But giving into the Lesser Self, making an excuse, is a tragedy.

#5 - Metrics vs. No Metrics - If metrics weren't necessary, then professional sports leagues wouldn't keep score. And players wouldn't seek to improve their stats. But they are essential because the scoreboard and stats don't lie. If you hit .200 in baseball, then guess what? You can't argue or brag about how good of a hitter you are. If you hit .300, your success as a hitter is evident. We track metrics to track progress. But also, to measure the effectiveness of our Regimen + Intensity. GRIT, just for GRIT's sake, is nothing but personal abuse. When GRIT becomes "Intelligent GRIT" though, through experimentation and testing different optimization strategies, to improve performance. That is how the average player becomes elite and sustains his dominance. There are mental metrics. There are physical metrics. There are Intensity metrics. There are time metrics. There are business metrics. There are relationship metrics. Without creating and tracking metrics, we could never improve them.

#6 - Integrity vs. No Integrity - The Heroic Self with GRIT doesn't ever have to worry about his or her Integrity being in jeopardy. If they say, "Default-YES; I am IN," then they're all-fucking-in with zero quit. <u>Their word is never empty speech. When it gets hard, they don't quit. When it gets inconvenient, they don't make excuses. When their teammate needs help, they're the first to jump in to carry the weight of their pack. Everybody says they have Integrity, but, if we're honest, damn few demonstrate it.</u> Most people are "ALL-IN," until, it gets hard. Or until, it becomes inconvenient. I get it, the urge to quit can often be great. But this isn't about doing a workout or missing a committed to deadline. This is about the Integrity of your Character. You told me you were "all-in." You said to yourself, "I'm all-in." Then, by your actions, you lied to me. You lied to yourself. Integrity is not about talk. Integrity gets demonstrated. <u>What makes Sloper and I such great Partners to one another, is that we won't quit on each other. He has my back. I have his. We have yours. We're committed. We follow-through. We don't talk about it.</u> Talk is cheap. A person with no Integrity, makes commitments and then breaks them. That is the Lesser Self to a tee. The Heroic Self, though, shows up. Every day, he is there. Putting in the work. Upholding his commitment. Not necessarily because he wants to but because he said he would. *That* is what *Integrity* is.

Remember: Our kids witness EVERYTHING - and they're constructing models to emulate. Which part of you, do you want to *demonstrate* to them? Lesser Self or Heroic Self, by executing these 6 Foundations?

Black or white.

This or that.

All or nothing.

If you make it a habit to always put the thing that you're deciding on, into this context, of black or white, this or that, no grey area, even the toughest or most inconvenient decision *becomes* easy:

<u>Which Character do you want your *kids* to emulate?</u>

Heroic Self - (**Emulate** *this*)	OR	Lesser Self - (**Emulate** *that*)
Default-YES	versus	Default-NO
Intensity	versus	Checking The Box
Suffer Together	versus	Suffer Alone
GO, NO-GO	versus	Random Check-Ins
Metrics	versus	No Metrics
Integrity	versus	No Integrity

Good Partners = Heroic Self

Partners *aren't* just business partners. They aren't just the Partners inside of your Open Source Community.

Partners *are* parents

Partners *are* spouses

Partners *are* friends

Partners *are* siblings

Partners are sons *and* daughters

Partners *are* employees

Partners *are* employers

In my LIFE and in my business, I don't have much patience for the Lesser Self – in any of these categories.

I have *high-standards* for myself.

I have *high-standards* for my wife.

I have *high-standards* for my kids.

I have *high-standards* for my parents and siblings.

I have *high-standards* for my friends.

I have *high-standards* for my employees.

I have *high-standards* for YOU.

I once heard Judge Judy say, "Rotten people are like rotten blueberries. If you don't remove them from your life, then like blueberries, they will infect and ruin the others in the container."

Said different, who you surround yourself with, matters!

A team of *Heroic Self*-people

versus... A team of Lesser Self-*dominated* people.

<u>Which Open Source would you *want* to be a part of?</u>

```
        Heroic Self - (Open Source)              Lesser Self - (Open Source)

        Committed Partners          versus       Interested Partners

        Full-time RE investor       versus       Continues to struggle
        Profitable online business  versus       Not so much
        Peak health & fitness       versus       Still chasing fads
        Leads a local movement      versus       Wishing they could
        Millions donated to charities versus     A few hundred bucks
        Compelling storyteller      versus       I'm not a good writer
        Enjoys 1000 True Fans       versus       Someone who can't inspire
        Documents the Journey       versus       Nothing to document
        Publishes a Book            versus       Nothing to publish
        Works together w/Partners   versus       Works alone

        = Shared Breakthroughs   (the outcome)   = No Breakthroughs To Share
        = Rapid Innovation                       = No Innovation
        = Growing Excitement                     = Growing Frustration

        1 - Does Hard Shit                       1 - Barely Gets Started
        2 - Doesn't Quit                         2 - Quits Quickly
        3 - Gets The Result                      3 - Fanaticizes About Result

        = Paid to Become Best Self               = Trades Dollars for Hours
```

Yeah, I figured. *Me, too.*

But even when you surround yourself with incredible people, their Heroic Self, inside of a community that operates as an Open Source, *shared* breakthroughs, success *still* isn't a walk in the park.

In this first 2 truths, we addressed how to "get paid" to become our best self.

      TRUTH #1 – Inspiring Others Is A Real Profession (Reader-Writer Relationship)

      TRUTH #2 – Leverage Partners (Business vs. Income)

In the next 4 truths, we addressed how to defeat the *Lesser Self* to get the transformative result, which, of course, is what creates the *demand* for the path you have traveled.

      TRUTH #3 – Proven Frameworks (Combat Failure; FODQ & Disease)

      TRUTH #4 – Sacrifice Is Required (Crispr; Editing "Defective" Behaviors)

      TRUTH #5 – Harness Compounding (Science of 1% Daily Improvement)

      TRUTH #6 – Open Source (Shared Breakthroughs; Rapid Innovation)

Each of these previous truths, though, have had to do with us *internally* not externally.

This next TRUTH is about the *external* challenge:

TRUTH #7
It's Called the Hero's Journey (For Good Reason)

It's damn hard to walk the *path* of the Heroic Self, and the *true* 5% most ambitious, like us, know this fact.

It *requires* commitment.

It *requires* sacrifice.

It requires "calling yourself out" on your *own* shit.

It requires *traveling* the Hero's Journey.

It requires *overcoming* the causes of FODQ; the Cycle of Misery.

It requires "genetic" engineering to *replace* "defective" genes.

It requires that you *write* the character *script* to defeat the Lesser Self.

It requires *doing* hard shit.

It requires *not* quitting on yourself.

It requires traveling the 1% journey to eliminate *improper* expectation.

It requires us to see *failure* as data.

It requires executing *frameworks* that force growth.

It's made easier by executing *proven models* from the start.

>It's made easier by operating *inside* of an Open Source to *share* breakthroughs.

>It's made easier by having *Partners* as teammates.

>It's made easier by *understanding* the path to have a *proper* expectation

>It's made easier by *becoming* your Heroic Self.

When you *choose* to walk this path, please know: Not everyone will embrace your decision to better yourself. You will be met with resistance. Those closest to us are *often* the greatest saboteurs.

We 5% → Don't fit in well *with* the 95% (the masses)

It's A Hard Road To Walk (And You Will Be <u>Met</u> With Resistance)

Nobody will fault you if you don't have the ambition or drive, or courage, to venture out on the Hero's Journey.

In fact, most people, the masses, prefer that you stay "stuck in the rut," so your ambition doesn't make them look bad.

It shouldn't be that way.

> But people are insecure.
>
>> <u>Your success gets interpreted *that you* must *think* you are *better* than them</u>:
>>
>>> After all, you have some money now - and they don't.
>>>
>>> You have some time-freedom now - and they don't.
>>>
>>> You have gotten in great physical shape - and they haven't.
>>>
>>> You're leading a local movement - and they're not.
>>>
>>> You tell your stories - and they think you're gloating.
>>>
>>> You have moved forward - and they're *still* stuck behind.

<u>It's an ugly game of *comparison* that the 95% play</u>:

> Our financially anemic friends *don't* want to see us make a bunch of money.
>
>> They don't want to see us *live* a financially successful life.
>>
>> They don't want to us *build* an ultra-profitable online business.
>>
>> Or become a *full-time* RE investor.
>
> Our 9-5 drinking buddies, too, aren't excited that we have escaped "the rat-race!"
>
>> They don't like that we can go on vacation whenever we want.
>>
>> Or, that we have *control* over our time = freedom.

Our overweight friends *don't* like that we have gotten into great physical shape.

They don't like seeing us eat healthy, *either*.

Or how much *energy* we have, when they're always tired.

Our peers or colleagues don't like seeing that our *"status"* has risen above theirs.

They're jealous of us leading a *movement* that donates to local charities.

They see our impact as, *"That should be me."*

Even our family (often) doesn't want us to share our journey or *tell* our stories.

They don't want to be the *characters* in our plot of life.

Or have to remember the *"full truth"* of the way things happened.

<u>I have *battled* every one of these.</u>

Who knew that by chasing your own highest potential, simultaneously, you would alienate others?

Step 1 – Ambition Is A Curse!

For a lot of years, I tried to find a way to bury my ambition six feet under. I couldn't figure it out.

Why couldn't I just be happy *doing*, and living the *life*, that others did?

Is there something wrong with me?

Am I ungrateful?

Do I not appreciate what I have?

Am I too focused on achieving the things that I don't have?

Am I focused on the wrong things?

Should I settle for the *life* that others seem to be content with?

Seriously, *what* is wrong with me?

<u>It seemed that no matter how hard I tried to make others in my life happy, their happiness was always at the expense of my own.</u>

It felt as if I was being asked to "put out my own flame," in order to light theirs.

My wife wanted me to "work less."

My kids wanted me to "work less."

My Mom wanted me to "work less."

Instead of watching TV, I'd sit on the same couch and *choose* to read a book instead. A book that inspired me and taught me and gave me ideas. And yet, still, somehow, I was demonized for it.

Seriously, can't you just relax?

Can't you just stop?

Can't you just be happy doing nothing for even one minute?

The answer is *no*, but why?

That was the question I couldn't answer, until I read the book: *FLOW: The Psychology of Optimal Experience*.

Be warned: It's a *dense* book.

But it answered, for me, that question above.

Why couldn't I just be happy, like everyone else, doing less?

> **The Way People Are *Wired*** – "Twenty-three hundred years ago Aristotle concluded that, more than anything else, men and women seek happiness." The problem is, happiness is something different to everyone. To the 95%, maybe happiness is the ability to pay their bills, be off at 5pm. Not have to work weekends. Take one vacation per year. With the freedom to BBQ. Watch football on Sunday. While playing fantasy sports and tracking their player stats as they watch. To me, though, *that* is a *life* of complete torture.

> **How People Like Me *Are Wired*** – "Contrary to what we usually believe, the best moments in our lives, are not passive, receptive, relaxing times – although such experiences can also be enjoyable, if we have worked hard to attain them. **The best moments usually occur when a person's body or mind is stretched to its limits in a voluntary effort to accomplish something difficult and worthwhile.** Optimal experience is thus something that we make happen. That we, as a creator, are responsible for bringing to life." Holy shit. That's it. That is what makes me happy. This is why I'm not happy, too, when I'm not building something of meaning. Or striving to achieve something difficult. I'm a creator.

Are people Genuinely Happy? – "Genuinely happy individuals are few and far between. How many people do you know who enjoy what they are doing, who are reasonably satisfied with their lot, who do not regret the past and look to the future with genuine confidence?" I don't know what that answer is for you. But outside of my entrepreneurial friends, my Partners inside of StoryAthlete – I don't know many genuinely happy people, satisfied with their lot, not looking back and are truly confident about the future. The fact that 1 in every 6 Americans is prescribed to some kind of an anti-depressant seems to support my observation. Thoreau and Benjamin Franklin were right. I see a lot of people leading lives of quiet desperation and publicly pretend to be happy. But in private, when they are alone with themselves, admit, they want more from their life.

DEFENDING HAPPINESS – The question: "When do people feel most happy?... What I 'discovered' was that happiness is not something that happens. It is not the result of good fortune or random chance. It is not something that money can buy or power can command. It does not depend on outside events, but, rather, how we interpret them. **Happiness in fact, is a condition that must be prepared for, cultivated, and defended privately for each person**." In other words, for us to be happy, we must 1) understand what makes us happy, then 2) design our life around that understanding. And then 3) we must defend our happiness from outside pressures and or attacks from others. I can't possibly serve the happiness of others if I'm not serving myself. But also, I possess the power to change how I'm serving myself, as the creator my own happiness, so, at the same time, I can best serve the happiness of others.

PURE Happiness = "WORK" – "There are people who, regardless of their material conditions, have been able to improve the quality of their lives, who are satisfied, and who have a way of making those around them a bit happier. **Such individuals lead vigorous lives, are open to a variety of experiences, keep learning until they day they die, and have strong ties and commitments to other people and to the environment in which they live**. They enjoy whatever they do, even if tedious or difficult; they are hardly ever bored, and they can take in stride anything that comes their way. Perhaps their greatest strength is that they are in *control of their lives*." That is me.

PURE HAPPINESS: I don't care "what I'm doing" as long as I'm being CHALLENGED. It's NOT that I love to "work" endless hours, I just love "pushing the limits of my mind and body," to expand my capacity.

This is about *how* I am wired.

Anything can make me happy *as long as* I'm going full-tilt toward pushing the limits of my mind and body.

Step 2 – Ambition Is My Gift!

Step 1 – *Ambition* is my curse.

It made me feel like an outcast.

Like I was a bad person. As if my only priority was to achieve "more."

```
And, when it was deployed in my life without care or
conscious thought, it made me extremely 1-
dimensional. All business. All the time. Causing my
relationships and health to crumble around me. It
wasn't: Mind, Body, Business, Relationships.
It was just Business.
```

Step 2 - My *ambition* is my gift.

Like most things in life, I have come to realize that ambition is a dual-edge sword. Until you understand what ambition is, and how it *controls* people like us, it feels like a painful disease.

Why can't I *just* be happy?

Why must I always *want* to achieve more?

The reality is, my ambition is what turned my BUSINESS into my life. Which caused my relationships to collapse around me.

But also, my ambition, once re-directed and re-focused, is what quickly turned my LIFE into my business.

Mind.

Body.

Business.

Relationships.

I spent a lot of years allowing my Business to become my life, and frankly, it nearly destroyed my family. A much better approach I have found, is to turn my Life into my business.

This time, instead of executing *solely* on sentence #1.

I wanted to *focus* on Sentence #2.

```
1) The game of money is a simple one. X's & O's. Add value, add
   wealth. That's the simple shit.

2) The game of LIFE. That is the true genius. That is the real game
   to figure out and play.
```

I love "business," don't get me wrong.

But the definition of business is anything that you "build, improve, and optimize to turn a profit." So why not make the optimization *of me*, my family, and my LIFE, the subject of that (new) business?

The first 6 TRUTHS in this book…

They have prepared you, through foundational knowledge and understanding, for this next step:

Step 3 – Design Your LIFE

The Hero's Journey.

If you're going to travel this path to become your Heroic Self, to live your envisioned life, then please be smart enough to at least design what you want to build into your happiness matrix.

It won't be easy to achieve, what you lay out in this section.

But that's the point.

1 – Do Hard Shit

2 – Stick With It

3 – Get The Result

This is the Hero's Journey.

Once you get the transformative Result, people will ask you:

How did you do it?"

What is your Secret?"

Remember:

```
1) The game of money is a simple one. X's & O's. Add value, add wealth.
   That's the simple shit.
```

How do we add value?

    1 – *Belief,* that it is possible

    2 – *Faith,* to take that critical first step

    3 – *Clarity,* go here, *walk* this path.

        There is nothing of more value than *Belief, Faith,* and *Clarity.*

        This is how we add wealth.

<u>In a minute, I'll share with you the 11 stages of the Hero's Journey, so that you know what to expect, as you harness your ambition, your *gift*, not your curse this time, to build your ideal LIFE.</u>

For me, though:

Here are some of the first thoughts that I wrote down:

    My ambition is my curse.

    My ambition is my gift.

    My happiness comes from being a creator.

    I feel most alive when I am pushing my mental and physical limits.

        I am not like the 95%.

            What makes them happy, doesn't make me happy.

        I am the 5%.

            Living a Challenge-Based Life is what makes me happy.

    I won't "put out my own flame," to light the flame of others.

    I refuse to sacrifice my happiness *to* create theirs.

        But I can change and shift my focus to create *shared* happiness!

And, I can harness my ambition to turn my LIFE into my business.

My ambition can be *applied* to achieve any objective.

For people like me, Work-Life Balance doesn't work.

Flawed concept.

Failed model.

Work-Life Integration, does.

Life *is* Business. Business *is* Life.

They are not separate, they *feed* each other.

Mind.

Body.

Business.

Relationships.

<u>I wanted to take all of that ambition that lived inside of me. And I wanted to design a *Life* where I got paid to become</u>:

A better friend

A better husband

A better father

A better *Partner*

I wanted every aspect of my life to align.

No longer could my professional ambition, be tolerated, to be at odds with my personal ambition, to finally be in good health.

Also, to be the kind of Dad that I committed to be, when my kids were born. I didn't just promise to provide for them. I vowed to spend time with them.

And my wife?

She deserved the best part of me. Not the tired, exhausted, asshole part of me; after the 12-hours of work I prioritized to the business.

From me; she deserved better. She deserved more.

Like I said, I wanted every aspect of my life to align.

Mind.

Body.

Business.

Relationships.

I wanted to workout with my kids.

I wanted to workout with my wife.

I wanted to get *PAID* to workout with my wife and kids.

I want to get *PAID* to teach my kids about business, and life, and success.

I wanted to get *PAID* to focus on my health.

I was 40-pounds overweight. "Fat Ryan" was robbing me of my best life.

Fuck him.

I wanted it back.

I wanted my wife to be proud of me.

Not because of the income I made. *Who gives a shit?!*

I wanted her to be proud of me based on the person I wanted to become.

And because of the example I wanted to set for our kids.

From being *just* Mind and Business orientated, to being equally focused on all 4-dimensions:

Mind. Body. Business. Relationships.

If one is weak, then the foundation is cracked.

And professionally…

If this was something I could figure out, then this is something I could share with others.

Add value; add wealth.

Belief – that it is possible (to achieve the *same* transformative result)

Faith – to take that critical first step (to get started)

Clarity – walk this path (to defeat FODQ)

StoryAthlete, this Community, where our Heroic Self shares our breakthroughs with our fellow partners, is the result of me traveling my own Hero's Journey to prove it's possible.

Once I designed the path…

I wrote the character *Script*, and, from that point forward, the character had to obey what was written.

That was back in 2018.

SINCE THEN, WE HAVE HELPED HUNDREDS TO DO THE SAME!

The 6 foundations that force growth (*in* the Committed).

The *StoryAthlete* software.

This Community

Open Source – all of our training, systems, processes, and protocols.

Shared Breakthroughs.

Yes, you can have the lifestyle of a full-time real estate investor.

Yes, you can build an ultra-profitable online business.

Yes, you can lead a movement that *donates* thousands to local charities.

Yes, you can write your character script.

Yes, you can document your journey through compelling stories.

Yes, you can enjoy the financial security of 1,000 True Fans.

Yes, you can do hard shit.

Yes, you can stick with it.

Yes, you can get the transformative result.

YES, YOU CAN!
Get Paid to Become Your Best Self

Limiting beliefs are the result of our *Lesser Self* stories.

Stories *create* Beliefs

Beliefs *decide* Behaviors

Behaviors *determine* Actions

Actions are what *dictate* our **Results**

(Empowering beliefs, different results, are created by our *Heroic Self* stories)

DEFINED BY THE STORY WE TELL OUR SELF – StoryAthlete is not some training program or brand of t-shirt. It is a Movement of the story we tell ourselves. Success is based on our belief. Our beliefs are based on the stories we tell our self. If we tell ourselves stories of defeat, we destroy ourselves from within. StoryAthlete is a *movement* committed to changing that reality. We believe each of us is the Writer of our own Character-script. And, if our Character fails, then it's because we wrote for our Character a poor script. By changing the story, we change the possibilities.

I SEEK CHALLENGE – The premise is simple. When my mind is telling that I am "done," that I am exhausted, that I cannot possibly go any further. I am actually only 40% done. The human mind is an amazing thing. It both propels us forward and holds us back. It is always possible for us to draw upon that 60% untapped reserve of energy, motivation and drive to keep pushing my forward.

TRANFORMATION – As a StoryAthlete, I recognize that active change requires a massive amount of effort on my part. Unlike passive change, which leaves me at the mercy of the current, I must create the new reality that I want to see in my life. Live the Challenge-based life. Travel the 1% journey. Obey the character script. Stay the course. It's all within my power.

Here are just a few of the *life-altering* Transformations that StoryAthletes have created for themselves, by living a Challenge-based Life, and obeying the Character Script.

- Battled depression
- Defeated suicide
- Grown large businesses
- Controlled neurosis

- Lost 80+ pounds
- Suffered through marathons
- Destroyed the Inner Critic
- Got promotions
- Inspired the family
- Looked up to by others
- Failed and got back up
- Became a voice against abuse
- Stopped living a Lie
- Fought PTSD and won
- Thrived in being adopted
- Succeeded as an Introvert
- Recognized as a Leader by peers
- Overcame an alcoholic household
- Realigned priorities
- Had the courage to ask for help
- Was an unflinching teammate
- Stepped into the Fear
- Refused to be a victim
- Developed powerful routines
- Refused to be a statistic
- Started eating healthy
- Inspired family to eat healthy
- Overcame crippling insecurity
- Stopped needing to impress others
- Overcame a shitty father
- Overcame a shitty mother
- Wrote books
- Became financially successful
- Got back in-shape
- Regained energy and life
- Overcame guilt
- Took off the mask
- Learned to be vulnerable
- Stopped fighting about money
- Found Purpose
- Stopped being soft
- Came back from financial ruin
- Woke the fuck up
- Stopped being complacent
- Reconnected with spouse
- Reconnected with kids
- Escaped the need to be Perfect

Everyone wants to be financially secure and happy. But figuring out this Game of Life, to play it at its highest level, is a sonofabitch. Until our demons and past, are confronted, then conquered, it's damn hard to become our Heroic Self.

It's all these negative stories and beliefs, and sabotaging emotions, that get *defeated* by the Character script:

- Issues of self-worth
- Self-doubt
- Crippling insecurity
- Impostor syndrome
- Fear of failure
- Fear of success
- "I'm not good enough."
- "No one wants to read my stories?!"
- "I'm not interesting"
- "Who am I to think I can have a great life?"
- It sounds too hard
- People are going judge and criticize me
- I'm too old
- I'm too fat
- I'm too stupid
- I'm not pretty enough
- I'm scared of being humiliated and embarrassed
- I'm scared to be vulnerable
- If I hide, I'm safe
- "Who am I to think I can have *this* Purpose?"

So, *what* is stopping you?...

Whatever it *is*, use it as fuel...

Step 4 – Execute The Journey

The Hero's Journey (again, called *that* for good reason)

Prepared by the 7 TRUTHS in this book, you are ready to *defeat* your Lesser Self, and turn your LIFE into your business. No turning back. No chickening out. The decision is made.

There are eleven (11) stages to the journey.

Understanding each phase, is what creates a *proper* expectation. Some journeys can be completed in months.

Others take years.

Remember:

"Most people overestimate what they can do in one year and underestimate what they can do in ten years."

Also, remember:

Turning your LIFE into your business is quite simple

      Step 1 – Do Hard Shit

      Step 2 – Stick With It

      Step 3 – Get The (Transformative) Result

          People will ask, **"What's your secret?"**

              = You will say, "Here's how I did it - **Go here...**"

              = *Get Paid to Become Your Best Self*

You'll notice Step 1, 2, and 3, is the simplified version of the eleven stages. Once you leave the Ordinary World to enter the Extraordinary World, into the journey, then return home...

You will return home with the "secret elixir," as your *gift* to others.

"How?... *What* is your secret?"

Remember, our job is to do the hard shit, to get the transformative result, that creates *demand* for our designed path. Once we achieve something, others will beg to know our secret.

Add value; add wealth.

Belief – that it *is* possible (to achieve the transformative result)

Faith – to take that critical first step (to get started)

Clarity – walk this path (to defeat FODQ)

Traveling these 11 stages of the Hero's Journey is the only thing standing between you and turning your LIFE into your business:

1: THE ORDINARY WORLD - This is the world we currently live in. It's good, but not great. It's tolerable, but *not* enough. The Hero in this story, you, me, knows we are capable of more. For some time, beneath the surface, the current of frustration has festered. A growing dissatisfaction has strengthened as you *believe* you can do more. And, be more. But the decision to pursue your Heroic Self, and highest potential, has yet to be made.

2: THE CALL - Some outside event, like reading this book (or it could be internal), breaks in on the hero, alerting or even compelling him to take action. The decision is made to leave the Ordinary World behind. His current situation is no longer tolerable. For too long, he has sat on the sidelines. For too long, he has wished and hoped. Even prayed. To no avail, his situation didn't improve. His current state of "being" has become toxic. The Ordinary World is no longer habitable.

3: REFUSAL OF THE CALL - Despite hearing The Call, at least at first, the hero always balks. Decision and action must reach a boiling point. Before answering The Call, the hero has to muster inner courage. He is afraid and fearful. He knows he has no choice. He knows he must leave the Ordinary World. He hears The Call, but he hesitates. The relative safety and comfort of his current position convinces him to remain in the forest, protected, opposed to pushing forth into the clearing where he is exposed. His fear gets the best of him.

4: THE MENTOR APPEARS - Hello, Obi-Wan Kenobi! Or the mentor may arise internally, in a dream or a vision. At the point, when the pain of remaining stagnant is greater than the fear of moving forward, the hero (using the guidance of the mentor) is infused with the necessary courage to overcome his fear of launching into the unknown. With the help of the mentor, or Open Source Community, backed by his fellow Partners, not only does he decide to push forward, he acts. He leaves the forest for the clearing.

5: CROSSING THE THRESHOLD - Hero says goodbye to the familiar, sets out into the Extraordinary World. This choice to leave the protection of the forest, and into the clearing, leaves him scared, terrified, and vulnerable.

6: TRIALS & TRIBULATIONS, FRIENDS & FOES - Now, fully exposed, the hero discovers the Inverted World. "This isn't how it was supposed to be." At this point, he begins to question or even regret his decision to leave the Ordinary World. The Inverted World tests our hero using the Wheel of Pain; one trial, tribulation, enemy, and fear after another. The weak turn back and retreat, while the hero pushes forth. He is scared and terrified, but he refuses to go back. He leans on the character *script*, just as he wrote it, to *defeat* the Lesser Self.

7: PRIMAL ORDEAL - The hero enters the Lair of Evil, where he comes face to face with his "heart of darkness." This is his greatest fear. At this point, he arrives at his "All Is Lost" moment. The point in the hero's journey where he is "as far from his objective" as possible. The hero is out matched, in every way. Out-manned, and out-resourced. If he turns back, all is lost. So instead, the hero enters into the epic battle against the enemy. Sometimes that enemy is The Resistance that lives inside us, i.e., Fear, self-doubt, a lack of self-worth, crippling insecurities. Or, the enemy can be external; criticism, judgement, or attack from an unexpected source, i.e., friend or family member.

8: THE PAYOFF - Hero succeeds! But wait... It is never that easy. No hero just defeats the enemy and triumphs. By leaving the Ordinary World for the Extraordinary World, and by being tested by the Inverted World to prepare him for his battle against the "heart of darkness," at this point, the hero still has to return home. A final journey where, if he doesn't use what he's learned, and lean on his friends and mentors to support him, he fails in his quest to return as a hero.

9: GETTING OUT - This is where the Bad Guys rally. You fought your way into the Extraordinary World. Now, you have to fight your way out of it. Fear does not let courage win, easily. Humiliated and defeated, initially, the enemy is now strengthened.

10: RESURRECTION - One final, hellacious test. The hero "is purified by a last sacrifice." His sacrifice earns him a moment of rebirth in which, the initial internal issue that was tormenting him, is at last resolved. By defeating this final enemy, his Lesser Self and limiting beliefs, this enemy no longer has any power over the returning hero.

Add Value; Add Wealth: Traveling the Hero's Journey is how the Hero earns the value (Belief, Faith, and Clarity) that he can now *share* with others!

<u>The final stage of the Hero's Journey:</u>

> **11: A GIFT FOR THE PEOPLE** - The hero returns to the place from which he initially set forth. But he does not come home empty-handed. <u>He brings transforming wisdom; an "elixir," that he donates to the broader community, to save it and bring it peace</u>. In a nutshell, the StoryAthlete increases his capacity to be a Light for someone else who is in the Dark.

Step 1 - Do Hard Shit

Step 2 - Stick With It

Step 3 - Get The (Transformative) Result

People will ask, **"How?...** *What* **is your secret?"**

Add value; add wealth.

Belief – that it *is* possible (to achieve the transformative result)

Faith – to take that critical first step (to get started)

Clarity – walk this path (to defeat FODQ)

= You will say, "Here's how I did it - ***Go here…***"

= *Get Paid to Become Your Best Self*

<u>At the beginning of this book, I promised a proven *path* for how to turn your LIFE into your business.</u>

I have delivered on that promise.

But, as stated, I didn't write this book for you.

I wrote it for my kids.

<u>If you look back to the Hero's Journey, between stages 3 and 4, this is where the vast majority of people stop. Freeze. Never progress forward. They hear The Call. But then they *refuse* it.</u>

And because the *courage* never showed up because they *didn't* muster it.

The Mentor never shows up, either.

So, stuck in this place, at Stage 3, is where the majority carry out their life-sentence. Wanting more for themselves, their families. Knowing they're capable of more, but never answering *The Call* out of fear.

I wrote this book, as a *primer*, to educate my kids on the necessary steps they would have to take to successfully travel the Hero's Journey.

Before they can find success and happiness, they have to find courage.

They have to overcome *The Fear*.

This book is my music.

Some people sing.

I write.

On Netflix recently, I watched the series *Country Ever After* about Coffey Anderson, and his journey to become a successful independent country artist. No label. Just his *decision* and commitment to:

1 – Do Hard Shit

2 – Stick With It

3 – Get The (Transformative) Result

Fourteen years later, that's how long he's been at it, he is headlining his own shows and has a Netflix series.

He is nobody special.

He is not an overnight success.

I'm sure if you asked him, there were plenty of times when he doubted whether he could make it. The road is long. The journey is hard. Winning the mental game is the only path to greatness.

You are your greatest adversary.

The *Lesser Self* is the destroyer of dreams.

The *destroyer* of hope.

The *destroyer* of happiness.

The *destroyer* of relationships.

139

The Hero's Journey is *reserved* for the Committed.

THE CHOICE:
Being vs. Becoming

Whether it's *for* my kids or yours…

This is the message I have been called to deliver; *being* vs. becoming - to remain stagnant and fearful, wishing happiness could be easier vs. *becoming* by traveling the Hero's Journey.

It's going to be hard.

It's going to be difficult.

The belief and faith you have in yourself *will* be tested.

To make it even halfway through the journey, could require years of sacrifice. Enduring one painful setback after another. I want them to know, *this* is when the character *script* matters most.

It's in these moments of Darkness, *when* the Lesser Self thrives the most.

Being able to recognize that *defeating* voice is critical.

They have to be *able* to silence it.

Why am I doing this?

For *what* reason?

Why is this *so important*?

<u>Different than the Lesser Self:</u>

<u>The *Heroic Self* thrives on Purpose and mission. And having a *vision* for his Life bigger than himself</u>.

I am *going* to make it - (I know it will be hard)

I am going to do *this* - (even if the deck is stacked against me)

Here is why – (to serve *those*, to me, that matter most)

<u>So, please - Write the Character Script:</u>

What will yours read?

Living 'The StoryAthlete Way'
Defined by The Story We Tell Our Self

Whether you believe that you can or can't do something, comes down to the *story* you tell yourself.

If your Lesser Self writes the story, you will be *destroyed* from within.

If your Heroic Self writes that story, you will be *empowered* to defeat the Lesser Self.

<u>StoryAthlete *Partner!*</u>

I want, not just for my kids to know what it means to be a great *Partner* to others in life. But I wrote this book, too, to set the expectation of what I define to be a great *StoryAthlete* Partner.

The Heroic Self = A Good Partner

In your marriage.

In your business.

As a parent, or as a friend.

<u>If we allow the *Lesser Self* to creep in, we will be *destroyed* from within, along with the Relationships that matter most to us.</u>

So, thank you - for reading this book.

Learning about *Story*Athlete.

Mind.

Body.

Business.

Relationships.

<u>In these 7 TRUTHS, you hold the knowledge to successfully travel the Hero's Journey!</u>

Living *'The StoryAthlete Way'* gets applied to every aspect of Life:

StoryAthlete
Get Paid To Become Your Best Self!

Let me repeat, one more time:

I spent a lot of years allowing my Business to become my life, and frankly, it nearly destroyed my family. A much better approach I have found, is to turn my Life into my business.

Those 2 sentences:

1) ```The game of money is a simple one. X's & O's. Add value, add wealth. That's the simple shit.```

2) ```The game of LIFE. That is the true genius. That is the real game to figure out and play.```

Here's the funny thing about those two sentences:

If you focus on sentence #1, then making money is incredibly difficult.

If you focus on sentence #2, then making money is simply the by-product of sharing your transformation.

Remember, "*How* did you do that?...

"*What* is your secret?"

In this book, I have shared my secret.

The 7 TRUTHS:

To successfully travel the Hero's Journey.

The 7 TRUTHS:

To turn your LIFE into your business.

The 7 TRUTHS:

To get PAID to become your best self.

How Will You Use This 'StoryAthlete Path' To Add Value To The World?

Add value; add wealth.

Belief – that it *is* possible (to achieve the transformative result)

Faith – to take that critical first step (to get started)

Clarity – walk this path (to defeat FODQ)

> = You will say, "Here's how I did it - **Go here...**"
>
> = *Get Paid to Become Your Best Self*

Hopefully, inside this book, I have delivered those 3 things to you. *Belief*, that it is possible to get paid to become your best self. *Faith*, that StoryAthlete can help you take that critical first step.

And Clarity of what a *proper* expectation is as you travel the Hero's Journey.

It looks like this:

1) **The Ordinary World** is the current state of *Being*.

    a. Life is descent, but not tolerable
    b. Frustrated all the time
    c. No energy. Constantly distracted and unfocused.
    d. Minimal happiness
    e. Getting worse by the day

2) **The Extraordinary World** is the future possibility of *Becoming*.

    a. Lifestyle of a full-time real estate investor
    b. Financial security of having a profitable online business
    c. Leading a movement that impacts communities
    d. Transforming self and family
    e. Documents the journey into stories and books
    f. Inspires others

3) **The Hero in the Journey** is the character *Script* written by the Heroic Self.

    a. Decision
    b. Commitment
    c. Sustained Discipline
    d. GRIT
    e. Perseverance
    f. Never Quits

```
(If you don't CRISPR to operate as your Heroic Self, nothing can help you!)
```

4) *The Mentor* is the Open-Source Community to support you throughout.

    a. The Committed (*not* the Interested)
    b. Together (*not* Alone)
    c. Shared breakthroughs
    d. Rapid innovation
    e. Forced Growth: The 6 Foundations

5) *The Inverted World* is the 3 Negative Cycles that feed the Cycle of Misery.

    a. The Cycle of Staying Small
    b. The Cycle of Missed Opportunities
    c. The Cycle of Mistakes

6) *The All Is Lost Moment* is every time the *script* defeats the Lesser Self.

    a. Proper expectation
    b. 1% daily gains
    c. Compounded 37X growth

7) *The Heart of Darkness* is the mental game against *FODQ*; Cycle of Misery.

    a. Frustration
    b. Overwhelm
    c. Depression
    d. Quit

8) *The Payoff, Getting Out, Resurrection* is the result of *Sticking With It*.

    a. Do hard shit
    b. *Stick with it* – (through CRISPR & Defeating *FEAR*)
    c. Get the (transformative) result

9) *The Gift for The People* is the value you deliver; Belief, Faith, and Clarity.

    a. Inspiring others is a real profession
    b. Transformation drives *demand* for the path you have traveled
    c. Leverage Partners
    d. Business vs. Income
    e. Work-Life Integration (*not* work-life balance)

        i. Mind
        ii. Body
        iii. Business
        iv. Relationships

    f. Be a *Guide* to your True Fans

They will ask you, "*How* did you do that?"

They are desperate to know:

"**<u>What</u>** is your secret?"

<u>By simply transforming yourself, through traveling the Hero's Journey, you create demand for the knowledge you have earned through your struggle to *Become* something more.</u>

1) The Challenge-Based Life
2) The 1% Journey
3) Hard(er) to Kill: Mentally, Physically, Financially

So, in our Relationships, we can be "the rock" to those we LOVE!

My friend,

<u>YOU</u> WRITE THE SCRIPT

So, write it well.

Mind.

Body.

Business.

Relationships.

<u>DEFINED BY THE STORY WE TELL OUR SELF</u>

If your character fails in life, it's because you wrote for your character a shitty script.

To my kids, never forget *this* simple truth.

Take responsibility, always.

In life, you have nobody to blame but yourself.

Love,

-DAD

```
Thank you for reading this book. These 7 Truths are the precursor to
everything in life because without traveling the Hero's Journey, you
achieve nothing. The Lesser Self takes the wheel. Controls you. And keeps
you firmly stuck in the Cycle of Misery. Don't let that happen.
```

ENTER:
The Extraordinary World

NEXT CHAPTER: <u>DON'T</u> REFUSE THE CALL

```
                Mental toughness is a lifestyle.

                                        - David Goggins
```

This book is *The Call*. It has shown you *The Path*. Don't *refuse* The Call. Don't let your Lesser Self convince you that the safety, and comfort, and familiarity of the Ordinary World is a better place than the uncertainty and challenge that lies ahead by entering the Extraordinary World.

The *Lesser Self* will try to rationalize and justify the decision to remain stagnant. "I'm not ready. It's not the right time." Don't let that *fucker* win. The hero must enter the journey, or he can't be the Hero.

So, please. Pick up the pen. Write the character script. Defeat the *Lesser Self*. In 12-months, you will be amazed, and in disbelief, of your newly created life. It's hard. It takes courage. And it requires you to *defeat* the FEAR. But, armed with the *Truths* in this book, you have that power.

```
            Note: To fast track and guarantee your transformation, find
            a powerful Open-Source Community that aligns with your
            beliefs and with what you want to achieve; Mind, Body,
            Business, Relationships. And join it. This is how you
            access Shared Breakthroughs to rapidly advance innovation
            and progress.

Partner with StoryAthlete?

    Turn Your Life into Your Business

    Get Paid to Become Your Best Self

            - Real estate investing

            - Online business (complete product-line)

            - Peak health and fitness

            - Lead a Philanthropic Movement

            - A Powerful Storyteller

            - Life of Adventure and Excitement
```

HEROIC SELF: STORYATHLETE PARTNER?

> NO MORE. No more excuses. No more: "I'll start tomorrow." No more: "Just this once." No more accepting the shortfalls of my own will. No more taking the easy road. No more bowing down to whatever unhealthy or unproductive thoughts float through my mind.
>
> — Jocko Willink

The purpose of this book, as promised, was to show you how to turn your Life into your business & get paid to become your best self. But also, additionally, to find and screen for *new* Partners. StoryAthlete is a community that lives, breathes and practices the tenets of living a Challenge-Based Life.

We don't talk about it, we do it. We don't bitch or whine about "having to do something hard," we embrace the fact that we "get to do something hard." Everything in life that is meaningful, and worth doing, is hard. So, why waste time complaining when we could just get after it?

Instead of running from pain, why not expect it?

As I wrote in the beginning of this book, greatness is hard. Greatness must be earned. Greatness requires sacrifice.

I also wrote, "Although we're able to show *any* Partner how to become a full-time real estate investor. And, how to build an ultra-profitable online business. And, how to live in peak energy in the best shape of their life. And, how to lead a grow a local movement that donates hundreds-of-thousands to local charities. And, how to tell stories to build an audience of 1,000 True Fans..." The fact remains, neither me, nor Sloper, nor anybody in StoryAthlete, can help you to achieve these things if you're not committed to defeating your Lesser Self.

As your Lesser Self, I don't want to be your Partner. And nobody in StoryAthlete wants to be your Partner. You would have nothing to offer. And probably, would be a giant pain in our ass.

Nothing against you as a person.

But your *Lesser Self* sucks, just as does mine. Trust me, you wouldn't want to Partner with my Lesser Self, either. Not even I want to partner with that piece of shit. For years, he ruined my life.

StoryAthlete can provide you the blueprint. Give you access to all the tools and training and supply you with the Open-Source Community to support you and to answer your every question. But only your Heroic Self, as the writer of your character script, can choose to execute.

Please, don't waste our time. *Or, yours.*

I was serious, though. If you are sufficiently interested in becoming a StoryAthlete Partner, I will walk you through the entire business model we will provide you; the complete product-line, plus the software, the tools, the protocols, and templates, including the Open-Source community that makes getting the transformative result, from doing hard shit, automatic and certain. This offer still stands.

For the readers of this book. And for those who have followed my stories and content for years, I want nothing more for you than to shift your "way of living" toward getting paid to become your best self.

Mind, Body, Business, Relationships.

Life is too short.

Most people are so busy working hard to earn a living, they don't have any time to actually live.

That is what we call "a *Lesser Self* life." And the *Lesser Self*, who keeps people trapped in this reality, needs to die.

I didn't want that life for me. I don't want that life for you.

I spent a lot of years allowing my Business to become my life, and frankly, it nearly destroyed my family. So now, a much better approach I have found, is to turn my Life into my business.

Recall those two sentences: 1) The game of money is a simple one. X's & O's. Add value, add wealth. That's the simple shit. 2) The game of LIFE. That is the true genius. That is the real game to figure out and play.

Game on.

```
Note: I have no interest in selling you on this opportunity
to join StoryAthlete at the Partner level. But, if what I
written in this book resonates deeply with you, and you
would value being pushed and held accountable by the Heroic
Self of others, inside of the StoryAthlete Community, as we
push hard daily, and fight continuously, ourselves, to
become hard(er) to kill; mentally, physically, financially,
then I'm excited to walk you through our Partner model that
is changing lives.

Start here.

StoryAthlete.com/partner
```

RESOURCES: STAY CONNECTED

```
The most powerful narcotic is the promise of
belonging.

                                  - Kalle Jasn
```

U like Kalle Jasn, I'm not so foolish to think "the promise belonging" is the most powerful narcotic in the world. Because *belonging* is something we feel. It's not something we analyze consciously. When people talk about Tribes, they're talking about culture. When people talk about culture, they're talking about shared values. Shared beliefs. Shared convictions.

"I like the way this guy thinks."

"I like the way this Community operates."

Look at Donald Trump's presidency, as a politician. No matter how much he "promised belonging" to the people that didn't align with his values, beliefs, and convictions, he couldn't win them over. Belonging is not an *act* of promise. Belonging is an *act* of demonstration.

The way I live my life, does it match with the way you live yours? If I think like you and if you think like me. And if you talk like me. And if I talk like you. And if we share the same parenting-approach. And if we share the same core beliefs. Some of the same values. If we have equal ambition. Work ethic. Levels of discipline. Etc…

Perhaps, we share the same outlook and perspective on business, too. And we share the same success-principles.

Well, shit.

Then simply by me living my life and you living yours, should our paths ever cross, we will likely connect and bond and with each another, almost instantly. Relationships, although complex, are actually quite simple. A relationship is nothing more than a series of connections and shared experiences, extrapolated backwards.

If I have climbed Everest and if you have climbed Everest.

Well, *damn*.

That's a connection.

We both did it. We share that. We have it in common. It starts with one. Then two. Then three. Before you know it, we realize we tend to share a similar approach to life. A similar philosophy. And worldview.

Each of these connections, starting with one but then dozens, is what creates affinity, "A spontaneous and natural liking."

We say to ourselves.

"I don't know what it is about this guy?! But I like this guy."

For most of my entrepreneurial friends, I instantly developed this kind of kinship towards them. Because, in all the ways that the 95% could never understand me, or my work ethic, or my ambition, they could. They had walked a mile in my shoes. And I had walked in theirs.

This is belonging.

Either you *feel it* toward a person, a group, a tribe, a Community, or you don't. You can't promise it.

This is why, my friends, I put out content.

This is why, I wrote this book.

This is why, I have a podcast.

This is why, I write daily emails.

This is why, within the content that I create, I do my best to share the kinds of stories that demonstrate who I am, what I believe, the values I hold, that are important to me; across Mind, Body, Business, Relationships. So that, as a beacon to others, they will know who I am and what I stand for.

StoryAthlete

Hard(er) to kill; mentally, physically, financially.

The challenge-based life.

The 1% journey.

Mind, body, business, relationships.

You hold the pen.

Write the Character script.

Defeat the Lesser Self.

Travel (successfully) the Hero's Journey.

Return home with "the gift," which you provide to others, which has great value, as your contribution to the world.

That's *what* we do.

That's *who* we are.

If your belief system aligns with that. And if what I've written in this book aligns with your mission and goals, then here are the ways we can stay connected as we travel our shared journey.

Daily Email – www.StoryAthlete.com/fletcher

StoryAthlete Podcast – www.StoryAthletePodcast.com

Trainings & Classes – Our promise is to always over-deliver. *Always!*

```
REAL ESTATE INVESTING: Every entrepreneur should add real estate
investing to their business. I don't need to convince you of the
wealth-building power of real estate. It's well-documented. It's
well-known by everybody. But what is the perfect entry-point to
get started? Welcome to the Asset Control Specialist Class. It's
```

30-Day class. Where, if Sloper and I had to start over from scratch. No relationships. No funding. No resources. This is how we'd do it. Look over our shoulders. Follow along. Do it with us, as we do it. No more wondering where to start. Sign up: www.AssetControlSpecialist.com

ONLINE BUSINESS: Write this down. You succeed online by simplifying the complex. Most people never execute because they are bombarded and overwhelmed with information. The cure to this is to simplify the complex. Traffic + Offer + Storytelling = Financial Security. That's it. And the best way to simplify the execution of that formula is look over someone's shoulder, as they explain what they're doing, as they do it. Welcome to the 30-Day Traffic Tests Class. Instead of spending $3K (on each) to learn the two dominate methods to run FB ads, you can look over my shoulder as I pit them head-to-head against each other. Don't risk your money. Risk mine. This is a better way to learn. Online advertising can be hard but it doesn't have to be. Sign up: www.StoryAthlete.com/traffic-tests

HUMAN OPTIMIZATION: Living the Challenge-Based Life can be as simple as choosing not to eat for 2-days. If you've ever wondered about the health benefits of Fasting and Intermittent Fasting - join CJ Thomas, StoryAthlete's Certified Personal Trainer and Body Transformation Specialist, to learn everything you need to know about fasting & intermittent fasting to feel 10X better in just 5 days! Sign up: www.StoryAthlete.com/fasting

StoryAthlete Membership – Open Source Community for the 5% more ambitious:

GRIT: To rewrite the Character Script, to defeat the Lesser Self, the first and most critical ingredient you need is GRIT. No more fucking excuses. No more of that bullshit "I'll start on Monday." Someday Syndrome, my friend, is over. GRIT starts now. www.StoryAthlete.com/grit

INCOME: I want to do everything in GRIT, plus, I want to turn my Life into my business and Get Paid to become my best self. I understand the formula presented in this book and I want a Tribe to execute the Challenge-Based Life with across Mind, Body, Business, Relationships. I want to build a PIB: Profitable Impact Business. For a full walk-through of the program, go to: www.StoryAthlete.com/income

PARTNER: I want everything in GRIT + INCOME, plus, I want to be plugged in to the Open-Source Community at the highest level. Not only do I want to turn my Life into my business and get Paid to become my best self, but I want to Partner with StoryAthlete to create recurring revenue. Attend mastermind events. Access all Partner benefits. Proven models. Templates. Protocols. And the desire to Impact my community through philanthropy, and my loved ones, through documenting my journey on every front, is something that compels me greatly. I want it all. Mind. Body. Business. Relationships. And Legacy. For a full walk-through of the Partner program, go to: www.StoryAthlete.com/partner

ImpactClub® - More than $2 million donated to local charities.

LEAD A LOCAL MOVEMENT: This is a gamechanger for every reason you can already imagine. There are real estate investors and entrepreneurs who claim to be trusted, respected, who desire authority and differentiation, then there are those who demonstrate it with through their actions, commitment to impact, as they lead by example. After 12-months as an active StoryAthlete Partner, members can apply to open a local ImpactClub®. Where in doing so, they can donate tens-of-thousands to local charities each quarter. Partners are granted area-exclusive territories. www.ImpactClub.com

Have a question – Text me: 360-215-7589

StoryAthlete

A NEW WAY OF LIVING

BEING vs BECOMING
THE CHALLENGE-BASED LIFE
THE 1% JOURNEY
THE HEROIC SELF WRITES THE SCRIPT
MIND
BODY
BUSINESS
RELATIONSHIPS
DEFEAT THE LESSER SELF
TRAVEL THE HERO'S JOURNEY
SUCCEED

"I spent a lot of years allowing my Business to become my life, and frankly, it nearly destroyed my family. So now, a much better approach I have found, is to turn my Life into my business."

- RYAN FLETCHER
Founder & CEO of StoryAthlete

StoryAthlete® is not just a company, podcast, or brand of T-shirt. It's a movement of changing the story we tell ourselves. Success is based on our beliefs. Our beliefs are based on the stories we tell ourselves. If we tell ourselves stories of self-defeat, as our Lesser Self, we destroy ourselves from within. Wherein destroying ourselves, we hurt and torture those closest to us.

Made in the USA
Middletown, DE
15 February 2021